TONY KELLY

RED CARD

THE SOCCER STAR WHO LOST IT ALL TO GAMBLING

TONY KELLY

RED CARD

THE SOCCER STAR WHO LOST IT ALL TO GAMBLING

MEREO

Cirencester

Published by Mereo

Mereo is an imprint of Memoirs Publishing

1A The Wool Market Dyer Street Cirencester Gloucestershire GL7 2PR
info@memoirsbooks.co.uk www.memoirspublishing.com

RED CARD

ISBN: 978-1-909544-70-3

Printed and bound in Great Britain by
Marston Book Services Ltd, Oxfordshire

Contents

Acknowledgements

The fact that you're reading this demonstrates that I have now fulfilled both my dreams in life – becoming a professional footballer and writing my own book. It has been an exciting journey. Fortunately I have had a lot of help and support along the way, which is why I have a lot of people to thank.

I believe we can all achieve what we want with dedication, discipline and hard work, but we also need the support of our loved ones and people who care. Now my project is complete, I want to show my gratitude and appreciation to those who have influenced my life in a positive way. I therefore dedicate this book to:

The Kelly family – Mum and Dad, Patricia, Abby, Ian, Errington and Charles and especially my twin brother, Mel. As a family we have had times of despair and tragedy as well as success and achievement, yet we have remained strong and united. Without my mum and dad supporting my football from the age of nine I would not have achieved my dream. Not just my immediate family but the Kelly family as a whole are united in love – that includes nieces, nephews, sons, daughters, cousins, aunts and uncles. I am blessed with an extended family and the Kelly name will live on for years to come, generation after generation.

The late and much-missed **Alan Ball**, former Stoke City manager and ex-England, Arsenal and Everton player. We all have a dream and I was no different. If Alan had not taken the trouble to travel to Stevenage one wet, windy Wednesday night I might never have had the opportunity to play professional football. I was gutted to hear of his death in 2007, as I knew what a great character the football world had lost. Alan will always remain an influential figure in my life and I will always be grateful to him for the faith he put in me when others would not.

My children – my son Shane and my daughter Savanna. Shane is now 17 and Savanna 16 and like any parent, I hope they will both grow up to be successful in whatever they choose to do in life.

Savanna always has time to listen. It is important that she understands the path my football career led me down, as she now appreciates the battles I had both on and off the pitch. I know how proud she is when she looks at the photo of me in my Stoke kit on her bedroom wall, and that makes me smile.

Shane wants to be a footballer like his dad, but he knows the mistakes I made and the grave consequences I had to live with. I have warned him about the pitfalls, but deep down in my heart I hope that one day I will be sitting in the stands cheering as he struts his stuff. Time will tell if his dream is realised.

The bottom line is that if my kids want it badly enough they can achieve whatever they want.

My further special thanks to:

Sandra Drakes
Lou Macari
Malcolm Cauldwell
Mel (Omele) Kelly
Errington Kelly
Jimmy Neighbour
Coundon Cockerels FC
Stoke City Football Club
The Stoke Sentinel
Talk Sport Radio
The Coventry Evening Telegraph
The Voice newspaper
The PFA (Professional Football Association)
Mike Bagley (Stoke City FC)
Chris Newton and Tony Tingle at Mereo Books
Elly Donovan at Elly Donovan PR
Warren Manger (Daily Mirror)
Dave Wood (Daily Star)
Terry Cooper

Introduction

For years I pondered over whether I should invite the public, my family and my friends into the secret hell of racism, despair, depression, stardom, gambling addiction and ultimately self-destruction I endured during and after my footballing career. It was my daughter Savanna, my former girlfriend Sandra and my sister Patricia who inspired me and eventually triggered me into putting pen to paper.

My story is one of sadness and happiness all rolled into one. I wanted my family and friends to have a real insight into what I had been through and to share in my experiences as though they had been with me on my roller-coaster journey. The issues I had to deal with – especially gambling and racism – feature prominently in this story, as they are issues which are still prevalent today and have in recent months come to the fore.

I want my journey to be a lesson to others, particularly to the teenage professional footballers of today. Temptation and a big ego were demons I failed to conquer, so I hope my story educates youngsters in a positive way and ultimately ensures that they do not follow my path of self-destruction.

Being a professional footballer gives you the chance of fame and fortune, but you need to surmount many obstacles and make many sacrifices along the way. As you will see, I did not conquer all the obstacles, nor did I make all the necessary sacrifices. If I had been able to do so, perhaps my story would have turned out differently.

Growing up as a young black boy in the 1970s in Coventry was tough, to say the least, but no matter what, I continued to pursue my dream and my story. Although I am filled with painful memories and know I made countless mistakes, at least it shows that out of adversity can come triumph.

I have been to hell and back, and naturally I do have regrets. Of course we all make mistakes – it's how you deal with them that matters, and what you learn from them that determines whether or not you come out the other side with your sanity, dignity and health intact.

My family and my faith have helped me to find the strength, courage and insight to put my story in print. Without that support I might well have gone where so many others have gone before me – to the point of no return.

We live in a different world from the one I grew up in 30-odd years ago as a teenager, but I hope that by sharing my experiences I will help others to become more socially aware. I also hope to help parents, teachers and mentors to guide their children down a more righteous path to enable them to conquer the many temptations and obstacles that lie ahead, especially for all those 'wannabe' footballers out there.

My ex-girlfriend Sandra always said I should be a writer, as I was always writing love letters or poems for her. I would always be putting pen to paper.

Although my sister persuaded me to write my story after she had read the first chapter, it is my daughter's story I will leave you to digest. I was looking through some old football annuals at a car boot sale and reminiscing about players I had played with. She gave me an excited but rather puzzled look. She knew I had played with some of these stars for many years. She said to me 'Dad, if you played football for all those years, how come you're not rich and don't live in a big house?' She was eleven years old at the time.

I paused for a few seconds and then said, 'Babs, do you really want to know?'

'Yeah' she said curiously. And I explained.

It was at that point that my daughter began to realise the trials and tortures I had experienced as a professional footballer. Now it is time for me to share those experiences with a wider audience.

So get ready for the journey. And please belt up - it may be a bumpy ride.

Schooldays and soccer

As a boy growing up, I dreamed of becoming a professional footballer. I felt passionate about it from the age of seven. Coming from a big family (six boys and a girl) I was lucky enough to have a lot of support and encouragement with my football. My identical twin brother Mel and I were determined to become the best we could.

Mel and I were born on February 14 1966, and by 1974 we were playing for our junior school team in Coventry, the Templars. This was the start of my love affair with the 'beautiful game' which was soon dominating my young years.

Our early days were spent living in the Tile Hill area of Coventry, before we moved to Coundon on the other side of the city when I was nine years old. I remember constantly badgering my mum and dad to find out whether my new school, Coundon Junior School, had a football team. I was delighted when I found out it did.

You might imagine I must have been the athletic type, loving football so much, but not so – in fact I was very slightly built when I was a young lad and didn't have much to offer in height either. In later years my slender frame would become an advantage as my pace and agility became apparent, but back then I wished I could have been bigger and stronger.

Although I would mess around at football with the Templars, I first realised how much I loved the game when I was watching a match on television. I remember the day as if it were yesterday – it helps that the occasion still flashes up on TV from time to time. I was watching the 1974 World Cup and that magical Brazilian team, which included Jarzinho and Revelinho and many other superstars. Two things stood out a mile: one was their bright yellow jerseys and the other was the incredible skills they demonstrated. Their football had me on the edge of my seat with excitement and joy.

I had watched our own First Division teams on football programmes such as *Match of the Day* and *Star Soccer*, but this was something from another planet. In terms of style and skill Brazil were head and shoulders above anyone else in world of football, and as the years passed they gradually became every neutral supporter's favourite team. That's how much they touched the footballing public and how well their talent was appreciated, even though they did not actually win the competition that year.

So it was the 1974 World Cup that started my love affair with the game. All I wanted was to be the next Pele, Jarzinho or Revelinho.

Closer to home, my favourite English player at the time was Gordon Hill. Hill was an outstanding left winger for Manchester United in the 1970s. I loved his skill and swagger – just like the magical Brazilians – and it helped that he scored some spectacular goals at that time.

Having progressed into the Coundon junior football team, I was now looking to join a local Sunday League team, as I was aware that a lot of boys my age were playing Sunday League football. Luckily for me and Mel there was a football club called Coundon Cockerels just five minutes away from our new home, and they had an under-10 team. Dad approached them to ask if they were looking for players and if Mel and I could come training one evening. I don't recall how Dad broke the news to us, but it transpired that I was more than welcome to come down and see if I was up to the standard. I got very excited about that, as I really wanted to play more football and to play outside school.

On the evening of our first visit Mel and I were feeling as excited as we were nervous. Dad was getting ready to take us in his VW camper van. It was a cold and misty October evening.

'You two ready yet?' he bellowed out, as I hurried to finish lacing up my black Gola boots and we ran out to the van.

Mel and I chatted in the van as Dad drove us to the ground. What was it going to be like? Would we be good enough? How would we get on with the other players?

The training ground was only a three-minute drive from our house, so there wasn't much time to get rid of the nerves. The sight of the floodlights illuminating the misty air gave me butterflies. We parked opposite the Coventry rugby stadium on Barkers Butts Lane and climbed out, all kitted up in our respective favourite strip - Liverpool FC for him and Manchester United for me.

We couldn't wait to get out on to the training ground and get started. It might not have been Premier League standard, but the goals actually had nets, so to us they were pretty special. The excitement of seeing the ball whoosh into the back of that black netting was enormous.

That was the night I met Dave McLeod, a strict but friendly Scotsman who would go on to become an important figure in my early progression up the football ladder. He introduced himself to Dad. Dave was a short, stocky, slightly balding man. He spoke with a Scots accent, but it wasn't so strong that I couldn't follow what he was saying. He seemed to be well liked by the boys. He was very welcoming and demonstrated a warm, calm manner.

'I hope they're bloody gud, we need some new young talent' he said. Dad smiled proudly in response. 'You won't be disappointed' he said.

The main thing that stands out in my memory about that night was the cold. I had to pull my sleeves over my hands to keep warm, even though I was wearing two extra tops. Mel and I both used to feel the cold badly, and it was a cold winter that year.

There were about fifteen or sixteen lads there with us. Dave split us into two teams and we played on a half-sized pitch. Somehow the mist and fog in the air and the moist grass made it all seem more exciting and we were soon running round like headless chickens. I remember thinking that I had to score immediately, so I must have been a little too greedy. As the match went on I found scoring quite easy - a lot easier than I had expected.

After the match Dave took us through some passing and shooting skills. I just loved the feeling of seeing my shots slap into the back of that net. Dad stood on the sidelines shouting encouragement. 'Come on lads, let's get that ball!' I would hear him shout. That spurred me on to play even better. Dad was never far away when it came to my football.

The hour and a half seemed to go very quickly. I remember feeling quite sad when Dave blew his whistle and shouted 'That'll do for tonight'. I wanted to go back there again as soon as possible.

As we helped to retrieve the balls and put them back in the bag, Dave gave me a friendly pat. 'Well done you two' he said. 'I'm going to have a chat with your dad.'

Whatever he said to Dad must have been good news, because the next thing I knew we were signing up for the club. We could now look forward to playing regular Sunday League football.

Coundon Cockerels was well known as an

established kids' football club – if you played for them you were looked on as a serious team. They actually wore the Spurs home strip, with a cockerel knitted into the top.

We played our home matches at the Memorial Park, a massive ground which is still popular today. The Sunday Minor League was a very good league and a high standard.

After a few games for Coundon I knew that all I wanted to do was become a professional footballer. Mel felt the same. We were very close, though of course we would bicker and fight as close siblings always do. Being so close meant we never wanted to be apart, so Dave kept us together and we played as 'twin strikers'. We scored a lot of goals.

★ ★ ★ ★ ★

So by the time I was ten years old I was already football crazy. Playing a match on a Sunday morning was no longer enough. I would get home from the Cockerels ground at about 2 pm and go straight over to Radford Common to play with Mel and our friends long into the afternoon. Naturally Mum and Dad wanted us to do well at school, but they knew football was my passion and gave me all their support.

Even at ten years old I took a remarkably disciplined attitude to my game. I would always make sure my boots were gleaming ready for Sunday. I used to follow the same routine every Saturday night. First I would watch *Kojak*, then *Match of the Day*, and then before going to bed I would set out to clean my boots. I would fill a bucket with water and get a knife to scrape the mud off, as I needed it to get at the dry mud caked in between the studs. To finish the job I would get some dubbin and polish the leather until my boots looked like new. I got a great feeling of accomplishment when I looked at my nice clean boots.

I don't remember my older brothers being anywhere near as interested in football as Mel and I were, although two of them, Abby and Errington, were very talented. Ian, the eldest, and Charles liked football too, but not as much as the rest of us. Ian was into anything and everything and was very well liked and respected by everyone who knew him. At 18 he went into the Army and I didn't half miss him after that. Charles was very focused on school, although when he started work it was down the mines; the mining industry was still massive in the 1970s.

My first season with Coundon went well - so well that we managed to get to the League Cup Final. All cup finals for the Sunday Minor League were played at the Butts, a beautiful big stadium which to me was as good as Wembley. Kids, parents and everyone else locally knew this and they would plan it so that there would be three finals on the same day, so there was plenty of support for all the kids. Normally you would have under 10s, under 11s and under 12s one day and under 13s,

14s and 15s on another. I thought this was a great idea as it made it two fun days out for all the families.

Our opponents that day were a team called the Chapelfield Colts. They were playing in the old England strip, which was quite intimidating. Perhaps that's why they beat us 4-1. Strangely enough I don't remember too much about the match itself, but I certainly remember the score. I cried my eyes out. The only good thing about that score was that Mel was responsible for our single goal. Needless to say he talked about it all the way home.

As I walked up the steep bank that surrounded the pitch to collect my trophy as a member of the runner-up team I could see Mum and Dad clapping proudly. I felt sad that we could not have won for them. The trophies were very flashy and expensive looking, with player figures on top and heavy marble bases. But when I had blinked away the tears I began to realise that I had really achieved something to help my team to get that far. I treasured that trophy, as I have treasured all the medals and trophies I have collected since.

As we made our way home I remember thinking to myself 'I hope I get back here next season'. It was a day to remember.

It was when I started at secondary school that my football really started to take off. Mel and I followed in our brothers' footsteps by going to Woodlands Secondary School, which had a reputation as the 'School of Football' because it produced excellent soccer teams which tended to win all the cups. I had a wonderful time there, particularly in the early years. They put me in Smith-Clark House, where I had a great housemaster, Mr Tranter, a Welshman with a deep voice and an even deeper passion for rugby. This did not prevent him from appreciating my skills with the round ball, and he would go out of his way to praise me whenever he could.

My PE teacher, Mr Cauldwell, known to the family as Malcolm, was also a big influence. He played a major part in my football development. He was always there to support me and always willing to spend time chatting with me. It wasn't just me who benefited from his support but all of us. Ian, Charlie, Abby and Errington all had his loyalty and friendship. No matter what the problem, he knew how to make you feel better about it. It was Malcolm who first recommended me to the manager of the Coventry City Schoolboys under 12s team, and I managed to go on to make him proud as later I represented Coventry schools at all age levels. He can't have been a bad judge!

Although I loved Woodlands, I didn't like the fact that we first-years had to wear school caps. I could hardly get mine on over my afro-style hair!

Mum and Dad always made sure we had cleaned, freshly-ironed shirts and trousers and that our shoes were gleaming, so I always looked smart at school. I suppose this discipline was to make sure I stayed on the right path. It worked - at least, it did at first.

Being a first year at 'big' school did have its problems, and one of them was my introduction to racism. I had never heard the words 'wog' and 'sambo' before. I didn't really appreciate how big a problem racism was, or how hurtful it could be. Racism wasn't just an issue for me of course – it was rife across the city of Coventry at that time and no doubt in many other cities.

I couldn't do anything about the racist comments I kept hearing from the older boys in the fourth and fifth forms as they were too big and strong, but I knew I somehow had to stand up for myself. I would have to wait until I was a little older to do that, and when I did the consequences would be devastating.

It helped that there were two of us, me and Mel, so we could look after each other. We also had the support of our older brothers.

Once incident which happened at school will stay with me forever. I was travelling home one day on the upper deck of the school bus. There was an older boy on the bus with us called Sean Riley, who had the reputation of being a hard case and quite 'useful'. He was a tough cookie with a long nose and a muscular build and had a rugged stone-faced look about him. Although he was no taller than me he was much bigger in build.

By now however I had grown immune to fear and was getting quite hard myself. I was sitting with Mel on the bus when I heard a shout of 'Sambo' from behind. When it was repeated I looked round to see Riley with a couple of mates, laughing and sniggering at us.

For some reason I lost it. I got straight up and walked down the aisle to the back seat where Riley and his sidekicks were sitting.

'What did you say?' I asked him, in the most menacing way I could muster. 'Nothing' said Riley, but he was still smirking. Without hesitation I kicked him hard, once, right in the face, then walked back to where Mel was sitting.

There was a shocked silence for a moment. I don't suppose anyone had ever done that to Riley before. But I knew it wasn't over.

'Wait till we get to Pool Meadow you fuckin' nigger!' shouted Riley, clutching his jaw. Pool Meadow was the last stop, the bus terminal in the city centre.

Mel and I looked at each other. We were braced for a showdown. However scared I was, I knew there was no way I could back down now.

As we stepped out of the bus at Pool Meadow Sean gave me a shove from behind. 'Come on then!' he sneered.

With Mel looking anxiously on, I waded in. The moment we were out of the bus, all hell broke loose. Riley and I began to kick and punch each other to a standstill. After a few moments I looked down to see that I had blood all over my school shirt, and it wasn't mine. But Riley would not go down. He was a strong lad.

The fight spilled out into the middle of one of the bus platforms and seemed to last for hours. Why no one tried to step into stop us, given that it was four in the afternoon and plenty of people around, I have no idea. Mel knew better than to step in as he knew I needed to show I could sort this out on my own. I would need to do this in different circumstances later in life.

Eventually Riley got me down on the ground. Then he stood up, panting. 'OK let's leave it' he said.

I had the feeling that each of us had gained a little respect for the other. We had had a one-on-one and we both knew it had been a proper fight.

After that Sean Riley became a good friend – and he never used racist insults again. Many years later I bumped into him in a pub in Coventry. We had a good laugh about our marathon fight.

Football was starting to get a little more serious now and I had become quite well known around the school for what I could do with that round leather ball. When I played for the under-12s I scored on a regular basis, helping them to reach the Inter School Cup Final. This match was very special, and it was that tie more than any other that made me realise I really wanted to be a professional footballer.

Again we were playing at the Butts, and this time the match was a dream come true. We played Ullathorne and won 2-0 – and I scored both the goals. Needless to say I became an instant hero to my schoolfriends. This was my first taste of what stardom felt like. At this level the matches received press coverage, and I could not wait to see the report of the match in that night's *Coventry Evening Telegraph*. I remember bursting with anticipation all Saturday afternoon, as the final was in the morning and I was hoping a report of the match would appear in the afternoon. As the clock ticked towards 6 pm, the time the paper was due at the corner shop, Mel and I raced out of house and sprinted down the road as if we were in a 100-metre dash. I don't know who picked up the *Evening Telegraph* first, but I do remember crowing with excitement as we saw that they had printed a full report of our game. It described me as playing a 'captain's role', which made me feel ten feet tall. My two goals were described perfectly, as was my missed penalty (sorry, I forgot to mention that!)

Mel and I rushed home to show the paper to Mum and Dad, our brothers and sister and anyone else who happened to be in the house. They were all delighted at our success and I'm sure it made Dad very proud.

So now I had my first winner's medal. I very much hoped it wouldn't be the last.

The following Monday morning I arrived at school feeling a little nervous and self-conscious, because I was pretty sure Mr Tranter was going to mention the under-12 Cup Final in morning assembly, as he was always proud of any sporting achievement by the school. He didn't let me down. He told the whole school at great length in his deep voice about my two goals and how proud he was that a Smith-Clark pupil had scored them. I was feeling quite embarrassed by the time he finished, but at the same time it made me feel very pleased with myself. It also made me even more determined to taste more success on the football pitch, as soon as I possibly could.

CHAPTER 2

Playing with the grown-ups

As the ugly smell of racism continued to poison my world, I became increasingly desperate to escape the streets of my home city. Episodes of racially-motivated violence continued to break out, particularly around the discos and clubs, and it was at one of these clubs that an incident took place which has stayed in my mind to this day. It involved a family friend and a local man who went on to make a name for himself as a professional boxer.

I was now fast approaching my 16th birthday and beginning to frequent the city centre clubs and mixing with some of the older lads. One particular club we used to go to was called Tiffany's – they had them in several cities at that time – and Monday nights at Tiffany's became legendary. The club was in the heart of the city centre and on Monday nights it was packed to the rafters. If you didn't get there early you could be at the end of a very long queue. This was under 18s night, so it was my chance to meet up with friends from school.

Unfortunately, for me those Monday nights didn't always go to plan, and there was one simple reason for that – racism. There was one particular bouncer, a smug and arrogant man called Tony, who just loved turning me and my brothers away. I will never forget his smug face and the pleasure he used to take in sending his back out into the cold.

Everybody knew Tony did not like to let in too many blacks, and it wasn't long before his reputation caught up with him. On this particular night Mel, BJ and I were turned away at the door, as usual when Tony was on duty, and we had to take a long and embarrassing walk back down the spiral stairs as the rest of the queue looked on.

As we went down we passed Errol Christie, whose career as a middleweight boxer was very much on the up. I knew Errol very well as he was friends with my older brother Abby and I was mates with his younger brother, Simon. The Christies were well known in Coventry as a successful boxing family, just as we Kellys became known as a successful footballing family. Errol's dad was a builder and decorator who worked on my parents' house.

Errol didn't look too happy. As he passed it he muttered something like 'Let's sort this wanker out'. I just knew it was all going to kick off. Mel, BJ and I turned round and followed Errol back up the stairs to the main doors again. The three of us stood back and watched as he approached the bouncers. We had all got sick of the way Tony and his team of fellow meatheads were treating us young blacks, and we all felt something had to be done.

Well – something was definitely done. I watched as Errol and Tony exchanged words at the door. Tony was standing half in and half out of the door. I think he was a little bit afraid of what might happen if he stepped outside, because he well knew who Errol was.

Then, quick as a flash, I saw Errol's fist whip out and smash into Tony's face. I had never seen anything like this before and I just stared in shock as Tony's head whipped back. He slumped on to the ground, his cowardly fellow thugs rushed to close the doors and Errol turned and started back down the stairs. I remember thinking 'so that's what a boxer's fist can do'. I don't know how badly hurt the bouncer was but you can be sure Errol did some damage.

That was my first close encounter with Errol. I would go on to see him perform later at a more conventional venue, Wembley Arena, which is another story. Errol became senior ABA champion in 1981 and turned professional the same year, going on to win the European championship. He is in the Guinness Book of Records for winning the most amateur title wins. He has even written an acclaimed book about his life coping with racism: *No Place To Hide, How I Put The Black in the Union Jack*.

So you can see why I just wanted to get away from Coventry and its mean streets and somehow make my way in the football world. Mum and Dad were very supportive of me and my football and they made sure I wanted for nothing. Whether it was new boots or shinpads or school stuff it was never an issue, even though my parents were far from wealthy.

One thing they made sure of was that however much I wanted to become a footballer, I was never allowed to neglect my academic work. I thank them for that. Thanks to their encouragement and discipline I managed to pass all my exams, and those qualifications would stand me in good stead in the years to come.

My older brother Errington was by now making his way in the professional football world with Bristol Rovers, and it wasn't long before Mel and I were shouting out his name from the main stand at the Eastville Stadium. I don't recall the first game I saw Errington play for Rovers, but I do remember the electric atmosphere at those home matches. It really made me feel proud listening to the wild applause every time Errington turned another defender inside out. Boy, my big brother had some talent. I remember thinking that this was exactly what I longed to do as well, to be on this kind of stage in front of a crowd of thousands, embracing the adulation.

Back to the streets, and me and the lads. Apart from the racism I continued to enjoy teenage life, and it was around this time that I had my first proper girlfriend.

Her name was Anita Labourne and she had an older sister called Sharon, who I must admit I fancied even more. We were all into girls now and I would meet up regularly to play music and show off our funky moves. At fifteen going on sixteen I was curious about all sorts of things. I suppose I always wanted to be in the fast lane, so to speak.

Ironically, it was the fast lane that fuelled my curiosity, because I loved cars and I had no intention of waiting until it was legal before I started driving. Many of the older guys were driving around in flash cars and I wanted to do the same. Long before I'd turned seventeen I had had lessons with Errington in his new BMW, so I could drive, even though I was too young to have official driving lessons or to take my test.

So another mad plan was put together. I don't remember whose idea it was, but it was crazy. Between us, Mel, BJ and I decided to buy a car – at fifteen years old.

A friend of ours called Garth had a Ford Capri, a very popular model then, a sporty one in brown with nice alloy wheels. One day the three of us decided to travel to Leamington, about ten miles or so, to look at it. Although I had been nuts about cars from an early age, I had no mechanical knowledge. That didn't stop me from paying the £200 asking price for the Capri. Don't ask where we got the money from – my mates and I had been stealing from an early age and had plenty of cash. We used to take loose change from the changing rooms at the swimming baths, nick purses from unsuspecting shoppers down at the market, and take any other opportunity we could to do some petty pilfering.

Whether the price for the Capri was a fair one or not I have no idea, but at least the car got us back to Coventry without falling apart. I loved that car and it wasn't long before the three of us plus our friends Terry and Mark were cruising into the city centre in it and pulling up outside clubs such as Shades to pose like big shots. At 15 going on 21 in my sunglasses, Sta-Prest trousers, moccasins and silk shirts I was growing up way too fast, but I was having a great time, even though I must have looked like a pimp. I even used to wear a gold sovereign to make the girls think I was minted.

The cars didn't last long after the novelty wore off. I did collect a few fines for driving without insurance or a licence, after being stopped and asked to produce my driving documents. What a mug I must have been. Mum and Dad became increasingly stressed and angry as Mel and I got into more and more trouble and I think they began to look forward to the day when we would finally be out of their hair.

With many of my friends embarking on lives of petty crime and taking one-way tickets to prison, I was becoming more and more desperate to get a football apprenticeship. I was scoring goals for fun for my school 16s team and was aware that scouts were sniffing round. At sixteen I knew time was running out, and so did Errington. I will always be grateful for his help in kick-starting my football career.

The time had now arrived, not just for me but for Mel. One day I came home from school to be told by my dad that Errington was going to call to talk to me about a trial with Bristol Rovers. Sure enough, he rang that evening to say that he had had a word with Bobby Gould, the Bristol Rovers manager, and that he had agreed for me and Mel to come down for a trial period. You can have no idea what emotions I went through after that phone call. I ran around screaming the house down and (once I'd calmed down a bit) I managed to tell them the news. Excited as I was, I was also very nervous, as I had no idea what to expect or how hard or easy the trial might be.

Errington came home after his match that weekend in 1982 and told me everything was in place for us to travel to Bristol the following week. Mel and I talked about nothing else. We just couldn't wait. The plan was to train for a day or two and play a youth team match with a view to signing in July, at the end of the school term. This was my opportunity, as there were only a couple of months of school to go and I needed to sign for a club by August.

That Sunday evening Mel and I left for Bristol with Errington. We enjoyed the two-hour drive in his shiny new BMW (a blue one this time). As we drove down, a whole mixture of thoughts were churning in my head. How was it all going to work out? Could I really hope to make it into professional football? We chatted about football as we went; we had lots of questions for our big brother. We got to Errington's place late that evening and he put us up in his spare room.

I well remember arriving at the Rovers ground the next morning and seeing all the flash sports cars. There were MGs, Triumph TR7s and all sorts. Clearly these footballers were well paid. Not that I dared to ask how much anyone was getting - it would have seemed a bit cocky to give the impression I thought I could be joining them.

Errington introduced us to Bobby Gould, who had a Coventry accent like mine and spoke with authority. 'Hi lads, I hope you're as quick as your big brother' he said (Errington was known for his lightning speed). He gave us some kit and told us to get changed. We weren't about to argue.

The training ground was wicked, with a beautiful little pitch and nice changing facilities. As I stood at the side waiting to start training, I remember watching two senior pros practising. They were pinging balls thirty or forty yards to each other with amazing precision and control. When I asked Errington who they were he said it was Gary Mabbutt and Keith Curl. Both these men went on to have successful careers in pro football. If only I could do the same I would be a very happy young man.

The training went well and we were told that on the Wednesday we would both be playing in a South East Counties match against West Ham Youth. Unfortunately that match proved to be a lot tougher than we had expected. Although I managed to demonstrate some nice touches and felt I played quite well, it was not good enough for Bobby to offer either of us the two-year apprenticeship we had been hoping for. Naturally I was gutted, but it was just another disappointment I had to take on the chin. It did make me stronger and even more determined to succeed.

So that opportunity was gone, but in an amazing twist of events I was given an unexpected second chance, and again Errington was behind it. Terry Cooper, one of the heroes of the 1966 World Cup squad, had taken over at Rovers' rivals, Bristol City, and Errington asked him to give us a trial. It's amazing how when one door closes another opens. I was adamant that I was not going to fail another opportunity. A trial was arranged for August, just after I had finished my exams, and once again it was time to travel to Bristol with our big brother.

This time the trial match was with Mangotsfield United, who played in the Western League, the same league as Bristol City Reserves. The reserves were made up of youth team players and young professionals, because of the small squads clubs had in those days. I played as a striker with Mel and this time the old 'twin magic' returned. We both scored and I felt I was playing well enough to impress those watching.

After the match Terry congratulated me on my performance and said he would talk to us the next day at training.

Bristol City's ground at Ashton Gate was in a truly

magnificent stadium. The massive stands seemed to go on for ever and the pitch was lush and green. The changing rooms were enormous. There was a KitKat dispenser outside the home dressing room, and I kept going back for more – something that would later come back to haunt me.

The next day after training, Terry told me and Mel to wait in the dressing room as he was trying to 'sort something out'. At the time we had no idea what he meant and were shaking with fear in anticipation of what he might or might not tell us. We waited for about fifteen minutes, and it felt like fifteen years, but there was nothing we could do except sit there and stare round the room as we listened for his return.

At last Terry appeared through the dressing room door.

'Right lads, I've got some good news' he said. 'We can take you both on.'

Well, you can imagine my relief. Those words were music to my ears. I had made my first step on to the professional football ladder, and I had no intention of falling off.

It turned out that because of the financial situation at Bristol City at the time – they had been in terrible trouble and had in fact just gone bankrupt - they could only take me on as a YTS (Youth Training Scheme) player, so the Government would pay my wages and not the club. These YTS schemes were introduced to get youngsters into work and were very popular with employers. We were told we would be paid £25 a week and given accommodation paid for by the club.

So for two sixteen-year-old Coventry lads, life was about to change in a big way. I just had to work out how I was going to break the news to the 'crew' back home that I was leaving Coventry, possibly for good. We thanked Terry and then sat and waited for Errington come and pick us up. We couldn't wait to tell him the good news. He was thrilled for us, and we couldn't thank him enough for giving us this opportunity and helping us to grasp it.

Back home there were a lot of things to sort out, and we took our time preparing for the move and discussing everything with our friends and family. Somehow the news had reached the local press, and there was a big article about me and Mel and how we had been given the opportunity of a lifetime to play with Bristol City. I kept that article, and we still dig it out sometimes when we are in a mood to reminisce about those days.

Mum and Dad were happy and proud, as they well understood how much it meant to us to have the chance to play professional football. They made sure we were fully aware of the importance of the opportunity we had been given.

I did a couple of shifts over the weeks that followed down at the indoor market in Nuneaton, just to relax and take my mind off all the excitement. Mum had a stall called Carmen's Fabrics, which was doing good business, and one day it dawned on me that I would probably never see her again except on brief visits. After I left home I would always phone once or twice a week and write letters to let them know how her 'terrible twins' were getting on, but I missed them terribly and I'm sure they missed us.

All my close friends, Terry, Mark, Garth, Marie and Anita, told me that one day I would achieve what I wanted so much – it was just a matter of time and hard work. My great friend BJ was a little upset, but he was pleased for Mel and me.

As we prepared to leave Coventry behind with our family and friends, the crime and the racism, I wondered how it would work out. Perhaps it would all go pear-shaped, as thing so often had done for me. But I knew it was up to me to make a success of my opportunity and to make sure I never had to return to the dark, depressing streets of my home town.

Finally the time came to say my goodbyes, pack my things and move on to my new life. One sunny Monday afternoon Mel and I finally left home for the journey south. The next 18 months were to prove eventful, to say the least.

After we had watched the lads who were about to become our team-mates finish training, Terry Cooper and his assistant Clive Middlemass introduced us to them. Terry was a sharp-witted, enthusiastic and very likeable manager. He was obviously well respected in the game, although to be honest I did not realise at first how big a name he was. He had turned to management after a 22-year career during which he had played for Leeds United, Middlesbrough and Doncaster Rovers as well as both the Bristol teams, and had managed Rovers for a short time before moving to City. He really knew the game inside out. He had been a member of the legendary Leeds United side of the 1970s under Don Revie and played with the England team which won the World Cup. He was the kind of boss you just wanted to do well for. He spoke with great knowledge and authority in that quirky Yorkshire accent of his. He was of course having a hard time at City as they had had a disastrous run and had been relegated to the Fourth Division. Fortunately, 1982 marked the start of a recovery.

We were soon on our way with Terry to our new lodgings, where we would stay throughout the time of my contract. As we drove through the streets of Bristol I couldn't help thinking how different it was from Coventry, with its tall buildings, wide roads and countless bars and pubs. There were also more black people than I had been used to seeing in Coventry. In a strange way, seeing black faces made me feel more at ease. My experiences in Coventry still lingered in my mind.

When we arrived at my new home the first thing that struck me was the size of the house we were going to be living in. It was a newish place and much bigger than our little houses back in my home town. We were greeted at the door by a very attractive woman who Terry introduced to us as Rose.

'Hello Terry' she said in a warm Bristol accent. 'Omele and Nyrere, is it?'

'Yes, I'm Nyrere and this is Omele' I said nervously. Those were the names we were known by then.

As soon as Rose ushered us into the house we felt at home. It had all the mod cons and it was clean and tidy and smelt lovely. Straight away I knew I would enjoy living there.

Terry left us to settle in. When we were shown into the main front room we found another lad slouched across the sofa. He was introduced to us as Nigel Smith, another youth team recruit who was staying at the house. I immediately hit it off with Nigel and the three of us spent the next half hour chatting about Bristol and football in general.

My first week of professional football training was a real eye-opener. There were about 20 pros and 15 youth team players and we would train separately, except for some occasions when we would all be mixed up together. What stood out during training was the exceptional technical ability of all the players. I was amazed how cleanly they struck the ball and how often their first touch was spot on. I would learn different aspects of the game as time went on, like pattern of play and tactics, areas I was not used to. The senior professionals were very friendly and one or two would always take time out to offer advice.

I knew I had a long, hard road ahead of me and that Terry would be watching my every move. It had been explained to me at the outset that I would not only be monitored by the management on my performances in training and on match days but that my attitude and my behaviour at my lodgings were also being scrutinised. Rose the landlady was paid by the club to look after young apprentices who had come from outside the city, and part of that agreement was that she reported weekly on any misdemeanours and issues she wasn't happy about. Nigel filled me in on the likes and dislikes and it was clear I would have to be very careful not to step out of line or else!

I spoke to the guys back in Coventry regularly and found that one of the crew, Terry Belgrave, had taken his first step on the slippery slope to nowhere. He had been sentenced to a spell in Borstal, but still found time to send me post and keep me updated on his wild ways. I kept Terry's letters, as when I had a bad training day or just missed Coventry they would cheer me up and give me a good laugh.

My training and development on the football field were moving fast and I was progressing nicely, so much so that I was soon asked to train with the first team and senior pros, even though I was still only sixteen. Terry singled out me and a lad called Andy Llewellyn, and we continued to train with the first team on a regular basis. I must admit I was still amazed at some of the things the senior pros could do, but equally I felt I filled in quite well and was handling the step up more comfortably than I thought I might. While I was training with the first team at Bristol City, Mel was still training with the youth team. He was finding things a little tougher than I was, but he was scoring plenty of goals at youth team level. We were both hoping he would get promoted to first team training with me, but sadly it never happened.

There was a down side to my contract as an 'apprentice footballer' and that was that I had some less glamorous duties to perform as part of my development. They included cleaning the professionals' boots, cleaning and sweeping the stadium terraces, preparing training kit for the players, washing soccer kit and running little errands such as popping out to get a newspaper or fetch a KitKat from the dispenser in the corridor, just to show that you had the right attitude. I really hated sweeping the terraces, so much that I would offer some small change or a KitKat to one of the other lads just so I could swap duties for the day. If you think I was being lazy, you don't know just how desperately boring cleaning those terraces was. Doing that job also meant I wouldn't be able to get away from the ground until 5 pm, so it was a very long day. But the senior players appreciated what I and the other lads did and we would always get a bonus of a fiver at Christmas and birthdays. It may not sound much, but that was a nice little windfall for a 16-year-old in 1982.

The highlight of the week would be settling down to watch the first team on a Saturday afternoon. I would play in the youth team or reserves on the Saturday morning and then return to the ground to sit and watch the first team. That gave us such a buzz, and it was something I longed to be part of myself. The atmosphere at the home match was electric and I well remember the ripple of applause that echoed round the stadium when one of our players had a near miss or produced a good tackle or pass. My experience of watching the first team brought back memories of watching Errington at Bristol Rovers. I was determined to taste that buzz and excitement for myself.

At this point I was beginning to sense that something special was in the offing. My hopes were fulfilled that October. One Friday I checked the noticeboard in the corridor at the ground to see what the squad would be for Saturday's match. Clive Middlemass had suggested to me that I might be 'involved' this weekend. Not quite sure I knew what he meant, I looked down the list of players – and there it was in black and white at the bottom, 'NYRERE KELLY'. I had to look twice to make sure I hadn't imagined it.

The phrase 'a dream come true' is a terrible cliché, but that's exactly what it felt like. I really was going to be a member of the first team squad. A strange feeling came over me, as although I was naturally delighted I also felt numb. It didn't seem quite real. If I was picked to play at the ground I would be making my professional soccer debut in a real match the very next day, and I was still only sixteen. I have to say I was feeling as scared as I was excited. I was being thrown in at the deep end and I had no idea whether I would sink or swim.

Mel and the other lads were well chuffed for me. I called my mum and dad to tell them the news and I could hear their pride down the phone. I had only been with the club a couple of months, and no one, least of all me, had expected such rapid progress.

So my debut in professional football took place on October 16 1982. We were playing Hartlepool United away, and when I arrived at Ashton Gate with my friend Alan Crawford to take the coach north I had never felt so nervous in my life. I was dressed up smartly in a carefully-ironed shirt with tie and slacks – shirt and tie was the dress code on match days for all players and you did not dare to break it, or you would find yourself out of pocket on payday.

The sheer magnitude of the occasion was starting to affect me and as we boarded the coach to Hartlepool I remember feeling like a little boy lost. As I took my seat at the back of the coach I remember my heart pounding with nervous excitement.

The journey seemed endless. In those days there were no laptops, Ipads or mobiles to help you while away the hours. All I could do was listen to the radio, read the newspapers and banter with the lads, or just stare out of the window. I wished the journey could have been only ten minutes instead of three endless hours.

Considering I was in the company of a bunch of my friends, I also felt surprisingly lonely. I was not yet mature enough to join in with the banter and the camaraderie. Some of the younger pros did their best to make me feel more at ease, offering me words of encouragement and cups of tea and coffee. They could see I was scared out of my wits. This was one time when I really missed having Mel around, such was the bond between us. I felt lost without him. Such feelings are I suppose quite normal for someone who has grown up as a twin, but fortunately they would not hinder me in my development in football or in life in general.

As we rumbled along the motorway Terry would give me concerned glances from time to time from the front of the coach, sometimes giving me a smile or a thumbs up, and this made me feel he was looking out for me.

Finally we entered the town of Hartlepool, and I began to see little knots of Hartlepool United supporters making their way to the stadium, all kitted out in their team's colours of blue and white. The closer we got, the bigger the groups got, the tenser the atmosphere became and the more nervous I felt.

After what seemed like an eternity we arrived at the ground and it was finally time to get down to business. At this point I had no idea if I was going to be in the starting line-up or on the subs' bench.

Compared to Ashton Gate the stadium seemed small and run down and there were no huge stands like those at home, which surprised me a bit for a professional stadium. It was only later that I would come to understand something of the business side of the game and the history and status of clubs like Hartlepool. We squeezed through the narrow corridors and into the cramped away-team dressing room and I sat down and waited on tenterhooks as Terry named the starting line-up. Strangely enough, I didn't feel too upset when he listed me as one of the subs. Part of me thought I would never last a full 90 minutes at this level.

When we ran out for the warm-up I finally realised that this was the big time. The stadium was already half full and I could sense the atmosphere building up. The small band of Bristol City supporters gave me a generous round of applause as I stepped on to the pitch (which by the way was not the greatest surface compared to the near-bowling green we enjoyed back at Ashton Gate).

Naturally I dreamed of racing out on to the pitch in the last few minutes of the match and saving the day at the eleventh hour with a glorious goal, but as debuts go mine, to be honest, was pretty forgettable. At least I did get to play in the second half, and I did enough in my 20 minutes on the pitch to keep my place in the first team squad even though we drew 1-1. I must admit though that I think the occasion got the better of me and I didn't do myself justice. It all seemed to go by so fast. The football was quicker and slicker than the youth team games I was used to and I found it physically tough, as I was up against grown men, guys who took no prisoners.

Terry and the senior pros had kind words for me afterwards, which no doubt was to keep my confidence up and make sure I would be ready for the next time I was picked for the first team. But I was proud of my 20 minutes of fame and the chance to show my pace, and it was an episode which would stand me good stead in the future.

It was a long haul back to Bristol, and as soon as I climbed back into the coach I was off to the land of nod. I didn't wake up until we got back to Ashton Gate. My professional debut was over, and my overriding feeling was that although I felt satisfied with my performance, I knew there was room for improvement.

Later I made a remarkable discovery – At 16 years and 244 days I had been the youngest-ever player to play for the first team. This was reported in the local press. My record would stand for many a year, and I am proud of it to this day.

As I continued with the daily grind of training and duties around the ground my thoughts turned to the coming weekend, because my friend BJ was due to come down from Coventry. Mel, BJ and I had arranged to go to a concert with the band Shalamar in the city centre and I was counting the days, as I couldn't wait. Shalamar was my favourite band back then. The band's Jeffrey Daniel was the first artist to perform the 'moon walk' – Michael Jackson didn't invent it, as everyone thinks. I was so into Shalamar that I had my hair straightened just like Jeffrey's, all sleek and shiny, which the girls used to love.

Because I was staying in club lodgings there were certain house rules I had to adhere to, and Rose, nice as she was, was very strict about them. Under no circumstances were friends, let alone girls, allowed to stay overnight. There was no smoking, and breakfast and dinner were served to a rigid timetable. The problem was that with us being so young there wasn't much cash around. There was no way BJ could afford to stay in a hotel, and there was no room at the lodgings even if Rose allowed him to stay there. But teenagers being teenagers, we just went with the flow and decided to worry about sleeping accommodation later.

Mel and I met BJ at the railway station and we made our way to where the concert was being held. I'm pretty sure it was my first experience of a live gig and it was absolutely amazing. They belted out all the tracks I loved and the now famous moon walk was the highlight. Everyone was trying to learn it, but without much success.

With the concert finished, we now faced a dilemma. Would BJ sleep in the car, or would we try to smuggle him into our lodgings? Having left my criminal activities in Coventry behind, I convinced him that it would be fine in the house as long as he kept quiet. It was around 1 am when we got back to the house, and all the lights were out, a good sign. When I opened the front door I could see Rose had gone to bed, and Nigel had gone away to see his parents, so the coast was clear. Mel and I had single beds, which I pushed together, and the three of us crashed out with BJ sandwiched in the middle. It was a good job he was a skinny little runt! BJ could talk for England and Mel and I had a hard job keeping him quiet, but a few right-handers to the ribs finally did the trick and we were soon all in dreamland.

In the morning Rose would always knock on the door and say 'rise and shine!' so we would have plenty of warning and there seemed no danger of our secret guest being detected. BJ was a free spirit who could always be relied to look after himself, so we just smuggled him out at the first opportunity and left him to find his way back to the station. It had been great having him down and as far as I know, Rose hadn't suspected a thing. I wondered over the next few days if she would start grilling me about the weekend, but she never did, so I presume she did never realise what had happened.

I played three or four more times for the first team, and then one memorable night I played for the youth team in the FA Youth Cup. This was at Plymouth Argyle, and we won the match 2-1. But the real story for us was that Mel scored one of those goals and I scored the other. Scoring became a habit after that - we continued to bang in goals regularly for the reserves and the youth team.

Unfortunately Mel's run of success petered out after that. In the run up to Christmas he was struggling. Although he was still scoring goals he had problems with other parts of his game and was also getting into trouble a little bit too often off the pitch as a bit of a 'Jack the Lad'. It was a very sad day when Terry decided to release him from his contract and he went back to Coventry.

After that I was on my own, though Mel was always in my thoughts and we used to chat regularly on the phone.

My next big night took place at Hillsborough stadium, Sheffield Wednesday's home ground. They hosted the FA Cup semi-finals in those days. I was fortunate enough to be picked to play in a League Cup match against Sheffield Wednesday, which took me further up the learning curve and gave me a taste of what top class Division One strikers can do.

One player in particular caught my eye. His name was Gary Bannister. Gary oozed class and became a big name in the 80s.

Mel tells me he remembers listening to the match on BBC Radio 2, and says how proud it made him and our parents hearing my name on the radio. We lost that match 2-1, but we put up a brave performance considering we were up against a top Division One side.

So there I was making my debut at 16, playing at Hillsborough and becoming the youngest-ever Bristol City player – what went wrong, I hear you say? I suppose all the attention and adulation I was getting on and off the pitch made me think I had already made it in football. How wrong I was. Around this time my focus started to slip. I spent wild nights out with the senior pros and started to adopt a bad attitude in training. I was getting too big for my boots, and it didn't go unnoticed by the 'Gaffer'. I wasn't getting so many smiles or so much friendly chat, although I was oblivious to it at first. They were obviously dismayed by my antics back at the lodgings – there were too many nights when I rolled in at half past two in the morning, and sometimes I smuggled girls in. I didn't always manage to pull the wool over Rose's eyes. I also used to leave my room looking like a pigsty.

This and my 'jack the lad' attitude all added up to a serious blow – demotion back to the reserves and youth team. I was told I was being sent to play a youth match against Shepton Mallet FC, down in the wilds of Somerset. It was a sharp reminder that I had not 'made it'. Not by a long shot.

Given the dire situation I was now in, it was clear to me that I was going to have to turn things round, and fast. So I did. We won that match 4-1, and I scored all four goals.

That earned me a return to the main squad, and on December 28 1982 I scored my first goal for City, in a 3-1 win against Hereford United. Mel and Errington came down from Coventry for the game and I was thrilled that they were there to witness my first goal at professional level. Errington was still at Rovers and doing well. He was vying with Paul Randall and Archie Stevens for a regular slot at the Eastville matches.

It was now clear to the staff at Ashton Gate that I had the talent to take me as far as I wanted to go, but as I was to find out all too soon, talent alone, in any sport, is not enough. As 1983 began I still wasn't being asked to play regularly for the first team, which was another reminder that I wasn't doing quite as well as I liked to think.

Mel was now struggling to find a new club which would take him on after his early release, and Dad had put in some serious mileage up and down the country taking him to trials, which unfortunately didn't materialise into any contract offers. My sister Pat was now living in London, and Mel understandably decided he had had enough of bumming around Coventry and went to share her flat in East Dulwich and start a new life in the Big City. He was so happy at getting away from Coventry. He found a job in security and signed up for a local non-league side, Dulwich Hamlet FC. I was pleased for him, as I knew he still harboured hopes of becoming a pro, just as I did.

They say you never know what you've got till it's gone, and this definitely applied to me in 1983. In May I was hit by a bombshell that I just hadn't seen coming. Although Terry and Clive rated me highly on the pitch, and I was well thought of by my team-mates and the supporters, there was a problem. One day Terry asked to see me after training. I thought that perhaps as it was the end of the season he wanted to give me a little pep talk and some advice for next season, but he told me very calmly and quietly that although I had all the ability in the world, my attitude was, basically, rubbish. He was releasing me from my contract. Like Mel, I was quite literally being 'sent to Coventry'.

'Son' he said, 'You will make it – as long as you sort your head out.' I now understand how right he was.

It came as a terrible shock. I thought I had done more than enough to at least be allowed to complete my second year, but Terry knew what he was doing. When I think back to the nights with the girls, the Big Time Charlie attitude and the antics at the lodgings, maybe I did need to grow up. I should have realised that in professional football it takes the right attitude and a lot of hard work to succeed, not just ability.

I saw myself returning with my tail between my legs to my family and friends in Coventry. That feeling of failure was awful, and it would stay with me for years. In the short term, at least it made me grow up quickly.

CHAPTER 3

Out on the town

Although I still had to come to terms with my sudden release from Bristol City, I was determined to make a name for myself in the cut-throat world of professional football. On my return to Coventry in the summer of 1983 I immediately contacted the local semi-professional clubs such as Nuneaton Borough and Bedworth United, in the hope that one of them would offer me an opportunity to kick-start my career again. The crew were still up to their old tricks, but they were very supportive and I was no longer quite so influenced by their criminal activities. In fact my mind was completely focused on making up for my débâcle in Bristol.

Mel was happy in London and I felt, and hoped, that at some point we would be reunited. Mum and Dad encouraged me to find some work, as things were tight financially and they still had a few mouths to feed at home, although Patricia, Errington, Ian and Mel had all left home for pastures new.

By this time Ian had been married to Michelle for about four or five years, so I didn't see him much, especially as he was always away with the Army and was regularly seeing action in Northern Ireland. When he was around I felt safe, as he was always a very protective elder brother and if I had any aggro with the other guys he would sort it for me, as they say. Errington was still scoring goals down at Bristol Rovers.

It was around this period in my life that I met my first real love. Her name was Tracey O'Neil and she brought a lot of joy into my life at a time of despair and confusion. I was not sure if I wanted to stay in Coventry – which I was finding even more depressing than when I had left – or if I should try to move to London to link up with Mel. Now that Tracey was in my life I decided to sign up for Nuneaton Borough, after a short trial. Their manager at the time was Graham Carr, whose son is now famous as Alan 'Chatty Man' Carr. Graham was another Yorkshireman who had an influence on my career. Although things would not turn out quite the way I'd hoped at Nuneaton, I was pleased that Graham made his way into the professional game as a manager and scout – he is still in the game today.

Nuneaton was a well-established semi-professional club playing at the highest level of non-league football, so it wasn't easy to secure a regular first team spot at the age of 17. There were ex-pros in the first team squad, along with some very promising players such as Trevor Morley and Eddie McGoldrick, who would go on to be fully-fledged professionals. Graham Carr seemed impressed by my potential but could not offer me the long-term contract I was after, so we parted company amicably and I moved on to Stratford Town. My brother Abby, at 21, was a star there at the time and he encouraged me to sign, saying I would be paid cash in hand and play regularly with the first team. So I took the plunge and joined.

I had a really enjoyable time at Stratford and found there was a decent standard of football, although at times I would get kicked all over the park! Remember I was still only 17 and playing against grown men, some of whom looked as if they had just been released from Pentonville, especially the centre halves. But playing at this level did toughen me up, and it was all good experience for the future. My attitude and self-discipline were improving. Tracey and I were still going strong and she would regularly stay over at Mum's, so my mum became quite fond of her. Tracey seemed to have a calming influence on me and her mum was a lovely lady too.

Another member of my family, my cousin Kenrick, was also trying to break into the big time as a footballer and had trials with Coventry City. He played a few reserve team games and did exceptionally well, so I was very surprised when he wasn't offered a contract. I can't say why it happened, but I felt politics had something to do with it as well as the lack of black players breaking into the game. Racism was still rife in society and maybe the hierarchy of these clubs were not comfortable at seeing so many black players making names for themselves. Although most professional clubs had one or two black players, many had none at all, so you can imagine the pressure a black player was feeling in the late 1970s and early 80s. We were often used as an excuse for vile racist supporters to vent their anger. Times have changed since and it's a fairer society now, thank God, but racism will never go away.

I was now banging in the goals for Stratford Town in the Midland Combination League, dating the love of my life (as I saw it at the time) and working as a banqueting porter at the Hotel Leofric in Coventry, so life was not so bad. Mel would come back home from time to time to link up with the crew and enjoy a night out.

On one of these nights out I had an experience I never want to go through again. We all met up and went down to Shades in the city centre. The night started well, with everyone in high spirits and me, Mel and the boys downing the lager like it was going out of fashion. Once the beer goggles were on we were heading for one of those nights when standards go out of the window when it comes to 'pulling'. Happy, hammered and horny is the phrase!

With the night nearly over we staggered out of the club and decided to invite a couple of girls back to my parents' place for a bit of you-know-what. As Mum and Dad were safely asleep upstairs we all made ourselves comfortable in the living room. Being young and randy teenagers we gave no thought to the possible consequences of our sexual conquests.

After a quick fondle on the sofa I and my new conquest got down to business. But my ignorance was to come back to haunt me in a way I had not expected. It required a trip to the doctor's and then to the chemists' to sort things out, and my little problem was something I have kept to myself to this day, as I would not wish it on my worst enemy. Thankfully I learned from such misdemeanours and always made sure I had change for the machine in the toilets, just in case temptation got the better of me again!

Unfortunately Errington's contract at Bristol Rovers had not been renewed, so he was on the market, so to speak. In a happy twist of fate his old manager at Rovers, Bobby Gould, had been offered the job of managing Coventry City. As a First Division club, Coventry was an attraction for any player looking for a move, and fortunately for Errington Bobby hadn't forgotten the impact he had made at Eastville Park. To my brother's enormous delight Bobby offered him a one-year contract with Coventry, and there was no way he was going to turn that opportunity down.

This period of the Kelly family's footballing history leaves a nasty taste in my mouth, thanks to memories of favouritism and racial bias. Errington became a massive hit with the Coventry reserve team, often outshining established First Division players, but he was always overlooked when it came to selection for the First Division squad. I remember going to Highfield Road stadium one Wednesday night to watch Errington play. What stood out was the reaction of the crowd. You could people whispering 'Who's that at no 10?' and 'Why isn't he in the first team?' or 'Surely he'll be playing on Saturday'. These comments were echoed by many, yet for some unknown reason the management kept giving other players the opportunity to shine at the highest level instead of my brother.

Although I was quite content with life, I still harboured hopes of being 'scouted' and getting my break in full-time professional football, and it was always at the back of my mind that at some point I would follow Mel to London. So after a successful season with Stratford Town and with the summer months ahead, it was time to party again. I made a few trips to the capital to see Mel and was pleased to see that he had settled in well. We would hit the London night spots and enjoy all the joys the city had to offer. What struck me most about London was the fashion – everyone seemed to take real pride in their appearance, and even if they were just wearing jeans it would be a smart and trendy pair. Unfortunately I didn't do much clothes shopping there because London shops were bit too pricey for me compared to my home city. I was still on a low wage working at the hotel and certainly wasn't getting a king's ransom at Stratford Town. Nevertheless I really enjoyed those weekends with Mel and my sister and I remember going to see the band Change with Mel and Tracey at the Hammersmith Odeon.

What a night that was! Change were a funk/soul band from America and at the time they were absolutely massive, so I felt privileged to get the opportunity to see such an élite band. The three of us were amazed at their talent and we danced ourselves silly as they pumped out our favourite tracks.

There were to be more nights out nearer to home that summer, as Mel would come home to Coventry and link up with the boys again, mainly BJ and Delroy, BJ's brother. We would hit the most popular clubs, Shades, Tamango's and Park Lane. There was an unspoken pecking order in Coventry when it came to who would go where – Park Lane, for example, was the Stringfellows of Coventry and was frequented by the 'money men' who had plenty of cash to flash, such as pro footballers and gangsters, while Tamango's was for everybody and anybody. I was respected by the older 'money men' even though I was only 18, because everyone knew who Mel and I were through our older brothers. That felt good, as it saved me from getting any hassle. Even if I was hitting on their girls I would just get a friendly whisper in my ear. The Coventry City players were regulars at Park Lane and in a weird way I knew that the attention and respect they commanded was just what I craved.

Shades was more a soul/funk club, and this was the one I enjoyed most. After all, I had been strutting my stuff there since I had been 16 years old. You would see gangster guys in their twenties cruising the place, usually with sexy blondes on their arms. They would strut around as if they owned the place and the gangster streak in me admired them, as it was clear that they wanted for nothing. Having said that, I knew most of these guys and I was regularly offered drinks and shown respect.

As I continued to party and ponder my future, Errington found himself with a dilemma at Coventry City. He had finished top scorer in the reserves, yet he had still not been offered a first team appearance, and now he was offered a further one-year contract at the club. Should he sign again for a manager who didn't have enough faith in him to put him in the first team, or should he accept an offer he had received from Peterborough United, who were in Division 4?

Errington and I still discuss that difficult decision to this day. In hindsight, perhaps it would have been better for Errington to stay with Coventry and hope his chance would come, but in the event he decided to accept a two-year contract with Peterborough. I was quite glad he had chosen the Northamptonshire club as it meant he would be a first team regular and get more money, which I felt he deserved.

I remember going to one of his matches early that season down at London Road, and it turned out to be a day that made me proud to be his brother. As I sat with Tracey and Mel in the main stand we saw

Errington scored a wonder goal. He cut in from the left touchline and curled a beautiful shot into the far top corner of the net with the keeper clutching thin air. I shouted for joy so hard I spilled my hot tea all over me. Errington got a standing ovation as he jogged back to the centre circle. After that it was obvious that he would be a popular player and he went on to become a real favourite with the 'posh faithful'.

I started the new season with Stratford Town, but the idea of moving to London was now looking like more of a reality. Mel had signed for Dulwich Hamlet FC and he was always pestering me to come and join him. He would tell me how nice the stadium was, how much he was getting paid and how he was living it up in London. I must admit I was jealous, as I was still doing a mundane job and my relationship with Tracey was beginning to flounder. She was still settled at home and in a decent job, and had no desire to start a new life in London. For my part I felt my time in Coventry was up and I needed a fresh start. We were both very young of course, far too young to think about any kind of permanent commitment, and to be frank we were not so deeply in love that we couldn't contemplate life without each other. So after my move, although we kept in touch, it became a long-distance relationship. And I can't help admitting that I was excited about the prospect of meeting all the 'talent' that London had to offer.

Mel called me one day to tell me that Pat had moved out of the flat and the council had agreed to let him stay on, which meant there was room for me, if I wanted to move in with him. I didn't need much persuading. Fate had dealt its hand and I knew it was time for me to leave my Coventry roots behind for good. Mum and Dad knew how close Mel and I were and I suppose deep in their hearts they wanted us to be reunited. I was 19 and halfway through the season with Stratford, so I knew it was as good a time as any. I told the club of my plans and they took the news well.

So all the Kellys were now doing their own thing and getting on with life in their own way. Charlie had been dating a lovely girl called Yvonne and Errington was loving life as a little superstar in Peterborough. Pat had left the flat to live in Enfield with her boyfriend Leeford. Although Abby was still making headlines for Stratford, he was now a father, and my niece Sinead was now four.

It was an exciting but sad time for me as I packed my bags to embark on a new life in London, a life that would bring me pain, joy, despair and many more emotions before I was through. After giving in my notice at the Hotel Leofric I got in touch with the crew and said my goodbyes to the mates I'd been having fun with since childhood. There were no tears or grand send-offs; we all knew our shared friendship was for life and we would never lose touch. That's how close BJ, Terry, DR and Mark were, and it's not as if London was on the other side of the world. And the city was nothing new to the crew, as they had all been there many times through criminal connections and had family in London.

It was time to realise my potential at last and to make a new life for myself away from the cobbled streets and the racism of Coventry. My mates were happy for me and my family were behind me, so I left knowing that whatever happened I was not planning to return. I just wanted to chase my dream.

With London being such an enormous city and so diverse racially, I was hoping racism would not be so much in evidence. I soon found that I had presumed wrong. Remember we were still in the 1980s, a decade which proved to be one of the darkest periods for racism. There were riots in Bristol, and who could forget the Brixton riots of the early 1980s? Unemployment was rising rapidly and with it was working-class discontent, with Mrs Thatcher running the country into the ground. In fact I was to witness racism in its strongest form in the most unlikely of places during my time in London. My experiences would leave me more shocked than anything I had seen in my home city.

The fireworks started, appropriately enough, on November 5 1985. My friend Errol Christie had now progressed well up the boxing ladder. He had reached a crucial point in his career, as he was now billed to fight in the British Middleweight title eliminator against Mark Kaylor. If he got through he would fight for the middleweight championship. In those days there was no satellite TV, nor even Channel 4, so Errol's appearances were all on the main TV channels. It made me feel proud to see a fellow black achieving such success and recognition.

The fight was publicised all over the place, and not just in Coventry but nationally and internationally. You may wonder why there was such massive interest in a fight which was only billed as a title eliminator, but this fight was much more significant than that. Unfortunately the bout was portrayed as black against white, although I suppose this was not surprising considering what was going on in England at the time. It didn't help that Mark Kaylor was a tough East Ender who just happened to be from West Ham, whose football team was notorious for its racism and violence. Back in the eighties the supporters of teams like Millwall, Chelsea and West Ham called themselves 'firms' and were little more than gangs of violent thugs who would travel the length and breadth of England to various football games just to cause mayhem, or as they would put it, to have a 'right tear up'.

Imagine the scenario – an up-and-coming black boxer adored by his home town and respected in the black community against a hard man from the East End, who is white and something of an icon to the West Ham faithful. It was a recipe for World War 3.

On the night, millions of ordinary members of the public in pubs and bars around the UK waited with fearful anticipation. Tickets were like gold dust, but fortunately for me and Mel, Errol sorted some out for us. I knew he had quite a few supporters coming down from Coventry in coaches, so I wasn't too concerned about being in the minority as far as support for Errol was concerned.

What a mistake that was. Errol had plenty of support from the Londoners too, but Mark Kaylor was idolised in West Ham and it was common knowledge that the team was one of the most successful clubs, pulling in 30,000 or more for their home matches.

The night captured the imagination of the British public and made boxing history, but for all the wrong reasons. It was the first time a boxing match had required a police cordon around the ring, for fear of what would happen if Errol won. Racism had reached a new low.

The hatred and racial tension struck me and Mel as soon as we arrived and we quickly began to fear for our own safety. The arena was packed with a sea of claret and blue and it was painfully obvious which side the British public were on. The atmosphere was intimidating to say the least, and soon after we had taken our seats we were beginning to regret accepting Errol's generous gesture.

Finally I turned to Mel and hissed 'Let's get the fuck out of here!' Unfortunately it was too late for second thoughts. We just had to pray the night would pass reasonably peacefully. But our worst fears were realised within minutes of the fight starting, when Errol knocked Kaylor down. I made the mistake of jumping up in jubilation, and looked round to see a group of white skinheads dressed in the famous claret and blue moving towards me and Mel. One of them struck Mel on the jaw, and the pack moved in. We were trapped between the narrow aisles.

I shouted to Mel 'jump!' We jumped about six or seven rows down, not caring about the consequences. Fortunately I managed to land in the aisle, only slightly injuring my left leg on impact and giving a spectator a sore back, but Mel was not so lucky. He gashed his knee badly and had to go to the medical room round the back. It was sheer mayhem, as we could hear the crowd getting fired up even more when Kaylor then knocked Errol down. It was turning into a war rather than a boxing match.

Mel was soon patched up, but we missed the rest of the fight as we decided it was more prudent to take a taxi and get back home. Unfortunately Errol lost the fight, but I can't help feeling he had more against him than just Mark Kaylor's fists. That remains the one and only professional boxing match I have ever been to.

As I settled in London, I stayed in touch with my mates in Coventry, but I did miss Mum and Dad even though I knew they were happy to see me trying to make a new life for myself. It's weird to think that there were no mobile phones back then, so if you did not have a home phone you had to walk to the red phone box on a regular basis. That was OK as long as it hadn't been vandalised, as it usually had.

I was starting to enjoy life in London and Mel and I were getting used to the night life and particularly the girls. We found we didn't have to do too much to chat them up, as the Coventry accent seemed to get the ball rolling on its own! I was intrigued by the Cockney accents and the stylish, sexy clothes the girls wore. I felt I had to keep up appearances and follow the fashion trends. This was not Saturday night out in Coventry any more, we were in London and I made sure I looked the 'biz' whenever I was out on the town.

Being such a pair of 'jack the lads', Mel and I were always up for some fun and games with the opposite sex. Being identical twins gave us the opportunity to have a lot of fun. I recall one hilarious night back in Coventry after we had been to Tamango's. Mel pulled a girl there and invited her back to our parents' house, so we were returning to the 'scene of the crime' after what happened there before. Our plan was for Mel to take his conquest upstairs to our bedroom to have his wicked way with her and would then make an excuse to come downstairs. I would then be ready and waiting to take his place!

After a while Mel came down with a big grin on his face, having told the girl he needed to fetch an ashtray, and gave me the signal to go upstairs for my turn. I crept up the stairs, taking care not to wake Mum and Dad. I hadn't been groping away very long when she suddenly bellowed out 'Put the fucking light on!'

I froze. Although Mel and I were almost identical we had different hairstyles. But it wasn't the difference in hair that freaked her out – it was because I kissed her. It seemed Mel hadn't kissed her once during their brief encounter, so she'd noticed that my approach was different.

'You fucking bastards!' she yelled, realising she had been taken for a ride in more ways than one. I quickly ran downstairs and waited for her to get dressed and join us. She came in yelling one obscenity after another, and she was not interested in hearing our explanations and apologies. She was soon out of the front door.

Fortunately for me and Mel, all-night rendezvous at our parents' house had become commonplace and they were used to it. I always had the feeling that Dad knew what we were getting up to but decided to turn a blind eye. I don't recall our parents ever interrogating us the morning after about what might or might not have happened during the night. With the number of girls who spent the night at no. 84 Three Spires Avenue, the moans and groans should have been enough to wake them up many times!

We laughed like idiots, but BJ did have the decency to go after her to make sure she got home OK. Not that that would have been much consolation to the poor girl. She was not the first to fall for the 'twin trap' and she wouldn't be the last.

Back in London, Mel was enjoying his security job and had landed part-time evening work in the bar at Dulwich Hamlet FC, a place which would soon become a regular haunt of ours. The 1980s were great times for music as well as football. I was a keen Manchester United supporter and Mel followed Liverpool, so we would always be looking out for their results on Grandstand. Mel bought himself a white Ford Escort

Popular (not that either of us had yet got round to taking a driving test) and we would bomb around London illegally with no thought for the consequences if we were stopped. That car was a nice little runner, but Mel eventually wrote it off. The way people drive on the London streets, it was hardly surprising.

It was now time for me to try to secure a contract with Dulwich Hamlet and join Mel. I was over the moon when they took me on at a salary of £80 a week. I already had my normal wage to live on, so I was beginning to feel a bit more comfortable.

Life was to take many more twists and turns as I continued to strive for the ultimate dream – becoming a full-time professional footballer.

CHAPTER 4

A little flutter on the gee-gees

I quickly settled into a flat in Dulwich with Mel and immediately found employment as a security guard with the same company he worked for. In those days you didn't need a licence or any particular qualification to do that job - as long as you were fit and presentable, with a few basic skills, there would always be jobs available in the security industry. I actually felt quite proud to have secured a full-time job, as I didn't want to be living in London as another unemployment statistic when there were three million out of work. I wanted more than that, and of course I wanted the good things in life.

My first day was pretty daunting, as I had to travel on the tube to some place miles away from Dulwich and I was not used to the Underground and felt very conspicuous in my new dark blue professional-looking uniform. I felt too self-conscious to wear my peaked cap on the tube as I wasn't sure how the Londoners would react, as I had discovered that their sense of humour was merciless!

I would work 12-hour shifts, which at the time seemed to drag on forever. Eventually I got used to getting through them by just thinking about the pay cheque at the end of the week. Mel and I were often working at the same site, and that was a laugh as we would constantly get people coming up to us asking if we were twins, and the resulting discussions would help to pass the day. It was interesting to see how intrigued people were about us being twins. You could see the genuine curiosity on their faces as they asked a barrage of questions.

It is quite special being a twin, and I always tell people it is very hard to know what it feels like unless you are one. In terms of having a best friend and someone you can talk to about absolutely anything, there's nothing to beat it.

The bond Mel and I had as twins would sometimes be an issue with our future partners, Jacqui and Sandra. We would call each other daily and Jack and Sandy would often say 'Why don't you two get married?', a joking reference to our constantly wanting to spend time together. Looking back I suppose they were entitled to feel pissed off, but the bond between twins can be so strong that even the woman in your life can feel excluded.

We now had our chance to team up again on the pitch, as Mel had arranged for me to train with him at Dulwich Hamlet, whose ground was just across the road from the flat. The manager was expecting me and had been made aware of my pedigree, especially my time playing league football with Bristol City. After a few training sessions I was offered a contract and Mel and I were once again partnering each other in attack for the reserves.

Dulwich Hamlet was a club with a lot of history which had connections with Crystal Palace and other big South East London clubs. As I continued to develop in the reserves I was soon promoted to the first team, which included players such as Andy Gray, Alan Pardew, the present Newcastle United manager, and Paul Harding, who went on to play for Birmingham City and Notts County. So you can see the talent there was in the side and what I was up against.

Mel also made a number of first team appearances before moving on to Corinthian Casuals, a famous non-league side in South East London. Although I missed Mel, I was happy at Dulwich and knew I was improving all the time, which was vital if I was ever to get into the pro ranks.

So here I was settled in London, enjoying my football, making new friends and working full time, but just around the corner there lurked a demon; gambling.

Back in Coventry the only kind of gambling I did as a teenager was the 10p slot machines, but in London the word took on a whole new meaning. Unfortunately, just a stone's throw from the stadium was a betting shop. And that was where all my troubles started.

Looking back now it sounds ridiculous, but I can hardly begin to describe the buzz I got from walking into a bookie's. Every time I saw those Mecca Bookmakers red and green stripes I felt I wanted to take up their invitation to go inside. I suppose part of it was that 'get rich quick' feeling – the belief every morning that THIS is going to be your day to hit the jackpot. Of course, it was fairly basic - there were no plasma screens or cosy seats like today. The staff would chalk up the prices on a blackboard while the punters sat around the shop on stools. Amazingly, there were no pictures to look at unless the meeting was televised - there would just be a commentary, which robbed you of the joy of seeing your horse win (if it did). The SIS real-time information system had not been introduced then, so you had to stand and sweat if you were waiting for a photo finish – painful!

The bookies' shops were generally full of what seemed old men (although they were probably only in their forties) smoking their heads off and pacing up and down hoping for that big win. I started to feel the gambling bug slowly kicking in when I got hooked on the fixed-odds football coupons. Not a weekend would go by without me having my customary 'accumulator'. I remember listening to Radio 2 (now Radio 5 live) to get the final scores and praying my accumulator had come up. Unfortunately there always seemed to be one team that would scupper my bet – a scenario that was to become all too familiar in the future.

We used to predict five away football results every Saturday or Wednesday, and one day Mel's bet was nearly up. He was just waiting for the Everton result. As this was a midweek bet Mel and I planted ourselves in front of the TV to watch Sportsnight, hoping that the 'Toffees' would beat Tottenham. To Mel's elation they did, one nil, with Gary Lineker getting the winner. I remember Mel bouncing off the walls in delight when Lineker showed his pace and sliced through the Spurs defence. He was in dreamland, having won £250 for a £5 stake.

The problem with gambling is that once you win, you get a real taste for it and you get dragged into a false sense of security, thinking you're bound to win again. I did have my successes, but of course a winning streak never lasts and you soon lose it all again. I'm sure that at this time I was in denial. I refused to admit, even to myself, that I had a problem. But the truth is, I was becoming an addict. I just hadn't realised it yet – and it would be a very long time before I finally learned to face the fact.

One day when I had just turned 19 and Mel was still sharing the flat with me, I had an experience that would burn a scar on my memory and stay with me for the rest of my life. It was something that made me realise how precious life is and how important it is never to take it for granted.

I enjoyed some great nights out with the Dulwich

players, and my friends from Coventry such as BJ and the brothers Trevor and Gerry would come up to stay with me and Mel. As I was working shifts in my security job, I would sometimes have to get up at 5.30 to get ready for work. My normal routine was to switch on the radio and listen to Horizon Radio as I got ready. One morning as I was listening to a track by a London soul band called Loose Ends I heard a knock at the door. I opened it without a second thought, to reveal a rather shifty, slightly Mediterranean-looking stranger standing there.

'Sorry mate, can you keep the music down?' he said in a Cockney twang. 'Bit early, innit!'

I told Mel to turn the radio down as I didn't want to upset my neighbours. But the following week my morning routine was again interrupted by a knocking, only this time it was banging rather than polite knocking. As I went to answer the door I felt slightly uneasy.

As I opened the door I was confronted by the same strange-looking man with a disturbing look on his face. He was middle aged and well built. He stood there dressed only in his boxers, dripping with sweat as if he had been jogging.

Before I could say a word I found myself pinned up against the concrete wall - and at the same moment I realised that he had the point of a knife pressed against my throat. My heart was racing and I just kept saying to myself 'shut up and listen'. From the evil look on his face, one false move or one wrong word and I was a goner.

'I told you not to make me come up here again!' he

raged. 'If I ever have to come up here I'll fucking kill you, you cunt!'

His eyes were bulging with anger and I stood there speechless with shock. I have never been so terrified in my life. I had heard stories about knife attacks in London, but I had never imagined it would happen to me, and I had never experienced such an outburst of rage and hatred. I stood frozen in shock as he swung round and stomped off.

My first thought was one of relief that I was still in one piece. My second was to go and tell Mel what had happened, so I got myself together and went into the front room, where my brother was still eating his breakfast, oblivious to what had happened. He knew something was wrong as soon as he saw the sweat pouring down my face. I suppose anyone who has just experienced what had happened to me could be forgiven for looking a bit pale!

'I've just had a knife put to my throat' I said. I could barely get the words out. I explained what had happened, and by the time I had finished, we both knew that we were going to have to go out for revenge.

When I told my sister about my ordeal she immediately told me to call the police, but I wasn't so sure. I didn't want to miss work while we gave statements and so on, for one thing. We weighed up the options and finally decided to keep it 'in house' as it were, and deal with our maniac in a more personal way, if you get my drift. That way Mum and Dad wouldn't have to know, and I really didn't want them going frantic with worry about us living in London.

The following Sunday morning, Mel and I were returning from the local paper shop with our *Mail On Sunday* so we could check the football results to see if our bets had paid off. As we strolled into the estate car park I saw a man in shorts washing his car in the sunshine. It was the man who had held a knife at my throat.

'It's him' I said to Mel. His eyes lit up. 'Come on, let's deal with him' my brother replied.

I wasn't going to argue, as I was still getting flashbacks from my terrifying experience and wanted this main properly paid out for my own peace of mind. We walked purposefully towards him. My heart was pounding and I felt rage welling up inside me.

As we drew to within a few feet of the man, he turned and recognised me, and his eyes went wide with fear. He raised his hands in a gesture of surrender. He began to mumble in terror, pleading with us. 'I'm really sorry about the other day, I was on the weed, I didn't mean it, I didn't know what I was doing, please mate, I don't want no hassle!'

He was begging. I looked into his eyes. He was sweating like a pig and shaking with fear. Now he knew what it felt like.

At this point the more forgiving side of my character took over. Although I was still filled with anger, I wondered if it was really worth the risk of getting into trouble for beating him up. I was in no doubt that his apology – and his terror – were genuine. Mel still wanted to beat the guy into the middle of next week, but I pointed out to him that we had already reduced him to a pathetic coward and that he would be most unlikely to try and mess with us again.

That was job done, as far as I was concerned. From that moment onwards we never heard a squeak out of him beyond the odd respectful 'Hello' or 'Good morning'.

Generally life in London was great, and I was definitely not missing what I had left behind in Coventry, although I did miss my family. My four other brothers were all doing well and Errington had completed his two-year contract with Peterborough United and taken an opportunity to move to Sweden to continue his playing career there. I was enjoying playing for Dulwich, but I was looking for a move to something more lucrative as the need to increase my earnings was becoming pressing.

One little problem we had lurking in the background was that we weren't actually paying any rent on the flat. Pat had been squatting there and we had simply taken it over from her. Inevitably the council caught up with us and gave us notice to move out. Pat invited us to move in with her and her boyfriend Leeford in their flat in Enfield, North London, so in January 1987 that's what we did.

1987 became a year to remember for many reasons.

Before I left for Enfield I managed to secure a contract with Mel's new club, Corinthian Casuals, which tripled my wages overnight. A great move, you might think, but the grass is not always greener on the other side and I was to find that out in a way that would change my life forever.

With my 21st birthday coming up later that year I was enjoying a new lease of life living in North London and teaming up with Mel on the pitch. Although I had dropped a notch or two in terms of the standard of football I was playing, I was happy, and I was beginning to make a name for myself on the non-league circuit. I have to admit that I was envious of some of my ex-colleagues at Dulwich Hamlet, as they had moved on to bigger and better things. Andy Gray and Alan Pardew had signed for Crystal Palace, and I couldn't help thinking that it could have been me.

Before joining Mel and my sister at their Enfield pad, I crashed at my cousin Rudolph's flat in Tottenham for a couple of months. Rudolph, Mel and I were very close and we would often 'rave' together as a group, along with Kenrick, his brother, my sister and her friends and Sandra, my girlfriend.

I met Sandra at a nightclub called Tottenham Ritzy on the famous Tottenham High Road. I'm afraid to say that this was another occasion when Mel and I were up to our 'terrible twins' tricks again, though nothing quite so juvenile as the stunts we used to pull off. We would often fancy the same girl, which happened one particular night at this club. We spotted two sexy girls on the side bar and parked ourselves opposite them. One was of mixed race and the other a tasty blonde. I made it clear to Mel which one looked like rocking my boat – it was the dark chick, Sandra. Unfortunately Mel had made the same choice. Considering we didn't even know yet if the girls would fancy us in return, it was jumping the gun a bit to put our twin plan into action, but that's what we did. It was a decision which was to have life-changing consequences.

We decided to toss a coin to decide who was going to be the lucky winner of the lovely Sandra. I won the toss – and that was how many happy years together began for me and Sandra.

Sandra Drakes came from a highly-disciplined background. Her father was from Barbados and her mother from Germany. She used to come and see me at Rudolph's flat in the evenings, but because of her father's strictness I had to walk her to the bus stop every night in time for her to get home by 11 pm. I was 20 by now for god's sake! Sandra was 19.

Apart from his disciplinarian attitude, I got the feeling when I met her father for the first time that he wanted more for his daughter than I could offer. I was returning home from training one Tuesday evening and stopped by to see Sandra for a short time. A tall, serious-looking man answered the door.

'I've come to see Sandra' I said nervously.

'Come in, she's inside' Mr Drakes replied, in what I

thought was rather a posh voice. He was welcoming, polite and engaging, but I felt he was expecting someone of a certain status, and as I sat there in my track suit and rambled on about football I could see he was not finding my conversation very stimulating. In fact, as my romance with his daughter blossomed, we went on to have a decent relationship.

Enfield proved to present a different side of London, one which would bring me new friendships and take me in new directions in football. I was now probably more settled than I had ever been since I had left home, as I was living in the beautiful house Patricia and Leeford had bought, felt settled at Corinthian Casuals and now had a new job as a postman based at Paddington Post Office. And of course I was head over heels in love with Sandra. It didn't seem life could get any better.

But one night that February something happened which would shock me and my family to the core and become a turning point in my footballing career. Forrest Gump said life was like a box of chocolates and you never know what you are going to get, and he was right. I certainly didn't see this particular chocolate coming and it most definitely had a hard centre. It was not an incident I could look back on with pride, but in the long term it did help my future.

I was playing in an away match for Corinthian Casuals, I don't remember who against, but it was a sunny day although only mid February. In fact it was my birthday, February 14. I was booked early on in the match, so I suppose I was walking a bit of a tightrope, but generally my discipline on the pitch was exceptional, so I wasn't too worried. Then as we got into the second half I was picked out by the ref for what I thought was an innocuous challenge. When he called me towards him I thought I was going to get a ticking off. But to my total shock and amazement, he produced a red card from his top pocket.

I stood and stared at him in astonishment for a moment, then asked him to explain his decision. I argued, then pleaded, but to no avail. He calmly asked me to leave the field.

It was a surreal moment. I just could not understand what was happening. I had not hurt anyone – it was a minor foul at worst. As I trudged off I remember thinking, 'It's my birthday and that prick has ruined my day'. I was trying to stay calm, but I could feel the anger welling up inside me and knew I was about to lose it big time.

As John Langford, my manager, put a consoling arm around me to usher me towards the bench, I flipped. I brushed him off and ran full steam ahead back on to the pitch towards the ref. With no thought for what I was doing, I pushed that referee with such force that he sprawled backwards on to his arse. The players and coaching staff of both clubs grabbed me and restrained me before I could do any more damage.

There was a huge commotion. I don't think anyone could really believe what had happened. As John marched me to the dressing room I remember thinking 'Shit, what the hell have I done?'

In football of course, attacking the referee is the ultimate cardinal sin, so I knew I was in danger of being banned from the game, something which would tear my world apart. The game was held up while the ref received treatment, although he was not seriously hurt.

After a bollocking from my manager – more sympathetic than it might have been in the circumstances – I was left to calm down in the dressing room while the match continued. I don't remember the score. All I remember is that from that moment the only thing I could think about was the punishment I would face.

I had to wait an agonising four weeks before I found out. I was hauled in front of the FA at Lancaster Gate, and although John pleaded my case as best he could I was given a nine-month ban. I suppose it could have been worse – they were well within my rights to ban me indefinitely. But not playing any proper football for so long would mean missing the rest of that season and half the next. That was an unbearable prospect.

As I sat down back at my sister's house my mind was all over the place as I tried to think of a solution to my dilemma. Then it hit me. I would join a new club under a different name.

Shocking as this sounds, it was the only way I could continue my drive to become a professional footballer, and such was my love for the 'beautiful game' that I was ready to do anything to achieve that – literally anything.

I discussed my plan with Mel. We agreed that if I joined a club in a different league from Corinthians and used a different first name, it ought to work.

As the season finished there was some great news for my home city – that was the year Coventry City won the FA Cup. As for me, I concentrated on keeping fit. Day and night I went road running with Mel while we tried to find the right club for me to join for the next season. Where I lived in Enfield there were three local clubs – Cheshunt FC, St Albans and Enfield Town. In July, the Cheshunt club, which was not in the same league as Corinthians, invited me down for some pre-season training.

Mel had decided to leave Corinthian Casuals too, as things understandably weren't quite the same for him there after my disgrace. He joined Enfield Town, a top non-league side playing the highest standard of non-league soccer. He was now dating a sexy young actress.

At this time I always seemed to be on the move for one reason or another. Back in those days nearly all the non-league clubs would pay players cash in hand, and as I was now without a contract I was determined to secure another deal. Pre-season at Cheshunt FC went very well and I soon negotiated a deal which would keep me sweet and also help me fund my increasingly disturbing gambling habit.

I still had to change my name to continue playing football in breach of my ban, so I decided to be known as Tony Kelly. Tony sounded more like a footballer's name than Nyrere. Under that name I signed for Cheshunt, and I never looked back. It didn't bother me to have to change my name for a short while, but I was relieved later to be able to resume the use of my real name, Nyrere. Of course after that I became known to the world as Tony, but my mum, brothers and sister still call me Nyrere, or rather Nez for short.

Sandra and I were enjoying happy times together. We would regularly meet up with Mel and his new girlfriend Jacqui, who he had met at one of our favourite haunts, the All Nations Night Club in Hackney. That was the place to go if you wanted to hear all the latest soul tunes, and it was legendary for its basement 'sweatbox', a hot, darkened room where only lovers' rock tunes were played – a slower style of reggae music. Girls and guys would sweat buckets together as they got 'down and dirty' smooching to the slow, sensual sounds. Lovers' rock was massive in the eighties and artists like Carol Thompson and Janet Kay were on a par with their male counterparts such as Freddie McGregor and Dennis Brown. Those nights at the 'Nations' were highly memorable and I would fall out of the place at six in the morning in a misty dawn with the sun coming up. This was London, so no 2 am closing. Most of the clubs would go on till daybreak – that's what I loved about the London night life.

At Cheshunt my football flourished, and it wasn't long before the scouts were flocking to Theobald's Lane to watch the new kid on the block. Errington was now settled in Sweden, and although I was happy for his success there, I felt his talents belonged in the English game and that his skills had not truly been appreciated by the people that mattered in the English game. People still talk today of the amazing talent he had. I recall a conversation between the Talksport presenter Adrian Durham and the Arsenal and England player Ian Wright about quick players. Adrian was a Peterborough follower and he remarked to Ian that Errington was the fastest player he had ever seen. I filled up when I heard that, as it made me realise that my brother had the qualities that should have made him a real star.

I finished the 1987-88 season as top scorer for Cheshunt. But although I was happy with my form and development, I did feel slightly uneasy about the fact that I couldn't use my real first name. As the summer of 1988 arrived I realised that my ban was over, but now I wanted to go on playing as Tony Kelly and to do it legally, so I made enquiries. My sister told me it was quite common for people to change or add to their names and this sounded like the answer. It would be good to stop feeling like a fraud.

So after a discussion with a solicitor, in July 1988 I officially became Nyrere Okpara Anthony Kelly. At last I had my identity back. My playing name would be Tony Kelly, just as actors have stage names. It was only in footballing circles that I was known as Tony, while my family and close friends would call me Nyrere, or Nez for short. I had often wondered where the name Nyrere came from and my mum eventually told me that Dad had picked it out of a book of African names – it is actually the surname (spelt slightly differently) of the late President of Tanzania, Julius Nyerere.

When you look at the names of my brothers and sisters there is an unusual mix. We have Errington, Abby (Abdullah), Charles, Ian and Patricia as well as me and Mel (Omele). Quite an assortment!

Sadly the gambling demon was now looming large in my life. In Enfield I had made some new 'friends' by the name of a certain William Hill and a Mr Ladbroke. And then Sandra landed a job working in one of these more modern, high-tech bookies! My fate was sealed. What had started as a friendly drop-in from time to time to see my beloved escalated to the point where I was watching the racing asking about singles, doubles, accumulators, lucky 63, placepots – all the wrinkles!

I was now firmly hooked. I just loved the buzz of that place, and with my girl behind the counter giving me free coffee and my wages burning a hole in my pocket I was in heaven – or so I thought.

I had now left the Post Office and through some dodgy dealings with my crooked colleagues I had managed to save enough to buy myself a shiny red BMW 316i. My passion for cars had never left me and I felt like a celeb bombing through the London streets in my gleaming Beemer. The BMW 3 series was every young man about town's badge of success in the 1980s.

I managed to secure a new job with Eastern

Electricity, which was more convenient in terms of travel as it was only ten minutes from home and from the Cheshunt ground.

In the summer of 1988, with a successful season behind me, I found myself in a position to move on once again. After a brief spell at Enfield Town under the then god of non-league football, Eddie McCluskey, I was offered a more lucrative contract at St Albans FC. I didn't have to think twice about making that move after meeting manager Dougie Parkin and being shown around the very impressive stadium. The pitch was like a bowling green. Considering they were only a semi-pro club they had excellent facilities and great support. Seven or eight hundred loyal fans would regularly turn out for home games – it may not sound like many, but that was a good turnout for a non-league side. I soon became established as a crowd favourite.

Sandra and I decided that it was now time to make our relationship more permanent, so we moved into a flat together above an estate agency. It was only a short distance from Pat's house, so I could still visit her regularly. Mel had moved in with Jacqui in Tottenham after a short spell staying with Errington in Peterborough.

Not a day would go by now without a flutter on the gee-gees. I didn't realise it at the time, but I was getting deeper and deeper into an evil addiction which had taken hold of me and was not going to let go. I had now learned the art of writing out complicated bets, and with my funds significantly bolstered by the £250 a week I was earning at St Albans I soon made Ladbrokes my second home. With the good wage I was getting at Eastern Electricity and Sandra's income we had plenty of money coming in – it wasn't about needing more. But that isn't how gambling works of course.

Putting my growing addiction to one side for a moment, life in general was looking more positive. Not just for me but for Britain as a whole. The dark days of strikes and economic depression with Britain sinking slowly to its knees were becoming a distant memory. There was still high unemployment of course, and it would take a lot more than a change of government to get rid of racism, but at least many people were coping better financially. The football world was changing rapidly in that respect, and after the dearth of black players over the past couple of decades it was great to see men like Noel Blake, Vince Hillaire, Mark Chamberline, Cyril Regis and the Stein brothers flourishing at the highest level. We were now living in a world where the club chairmen and money men were more open-minded and the culture formed by the ignorant, racist business types who knew nothing about football was becoming a thing of the past.

It has to be said however that we still don't seem to be able to appoint a black manager. There are many different opinions over the reasons for this, which I won't go into now, but I will point out how many black footballers have now distinguished themselves at the top of our profession as players and ask - why can't the experience, knowledge and commitment they have demonstrated be used to benefit football clubs at the top? The power men need to wise up and give some of these ex-players an opportunity to show what they can do. Now that I am looking in from the outside in the aftermath of a nine-year professional career I can see how little change there has been in the attitudes of chairmen and owners of English Football League clubs. This saddens me, as I know of so many black former players who have been passed over for management opportunities. Let's hope it changes soon.

So life for me was good with my income, my soccer, my lovely Sandra, my busy social life and my shining BMW, but contented? No way. I was still hoping and praying that a talent scout would come along and pluck me from obscurity, and that my dream of becoming a proper league footballer would turn into reality. I actually wrote letters headed 'Dear God' and put them into the bible Sandra kept at our bedside! At least my displays for St Albans gave me good reason to think my time might not be too far off.

The big opportunity began with a trip to visit Errington in Sweden. He was a fully-fledged pro and now settled there. It was a great trip and Mel and I much enjoyed the 24-hour ferry crossing. I couldn't get over the size of the ship, and there was so much to do on board. We spent half the trip in the so-called 'night club'. It was like any club you would find in London, packed with sexy girls, with loud music and a great choice of drinks. There was also a casino on board, but I hadn't tasted this game yet so my wad of krona was safe that time, at least.

Errington and I discussed what to do about my future and he advised me to write to a few Swedish clubs offering my services. I did as he suggested. A few days later I received a summons to a meeting with the St Albans management. I thought, 'Fuck, what have I done now?' But when I went into the office of the chairman, Bernard Tominey, I was greeted with a beaming smile.

'Great news, Tony' he said. 'We've had an offer for you from a second division Swedish club. They want you to go over next week. Are you interested?'

I sat stunned for a few seconds, my mind going back to my recent break with Errington and the sight of all those blonde Scandinavian beauties. Seriously, this news took a while to sink in. Bernard and Dougie proceeded to fill me in on the contractual details. They stressed that this was a loan deal between the two clubs and that I would be coming back to St Albans at the end of the Swedish season. This didn't bother me in the slightest as I still had my dream back home to fulfil. The Swedish season is opposite to ours, running from March to October with a break in July, so I was to spend the summer of 1989 out there. I would be paid £300 a week tax free and staying at an apartment free of charge into the bargain. Not only that, all flights to and from Sweden would be paid for, for Sandra as well.

And while I was still gawping in disbelief, Bernard hit me with yet more 'freebies'. All my breakfasts and dinners would be free at the club restaurant, and I would be given a Volvo for my personal use.

What a break! I couldn't pack my bags quickly enough. But first I had to tell Sandra the news, and although she was pleased for me and wanted me to accept the offer, I could see that underneath she was upset. I had mixed emotions too – after all, I was leaving my sweetheart behind, and it wasn't as if Sweden was just down the road.

Anyway, we agreed that the move was in my best interests, and of course she could visit me for a week or two at any time. I would be back in July for the mid-season break, so it wasn't so bad. My parents, who had now moved to High Wycombe, were pleased at my news, as were the rest of my family. But it was going to be a wrench parting with Mel as we were so close. He understood my reasons for going and supported the decision, not least because he knew I would be earning some decent 'wedge'. I went back to Coventry to say goodbye to my friends there. I remember writing a letter to Marie which she still has, 24 years later.

Now to sort out the travel arrangements with my manager at St Albans. There was no way I was going by ferry – I wasn't prepared to spend 24 hours on a boat again, much as Mel and I had enjoyed it on our visit to Errington, so they arranged for me to fly. With bags packed and goodbyes said, off I went to start my new life. That April day when I left the UK still has a special place in my memories.

Me and Mel aged 9 – I'm on the right

With Stoke City in 1990

Just after I signed for Bristol City

On arrival in Sweden, 1989

Playing for St Albans against Windsor & Eton, 1988

At 19, proud owner of my first BMW

Taking on Colchester's Peter Cawley in a match for Leyton Orient

Playing for Bury against Darlington, May 1995

Supporters' day 1995, with a
young fan

Celebrating our Wembley win
with my neighbour Gareth

Bursting through the Darlington defence in a match for Leyton Orient, 1996

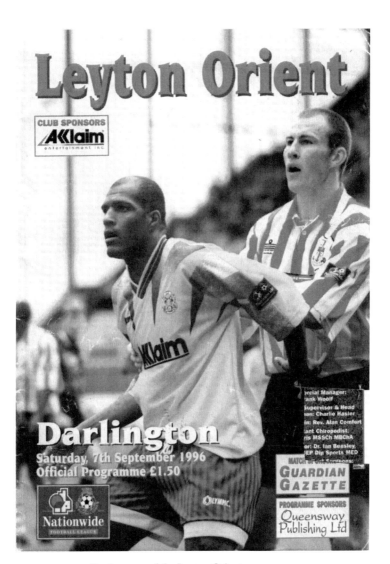

On the cover of the Leyton Orient programme

TONY KELLY

Born: Meridan, 14th February 1996
Previous Clubs: Bristol City (youngest ever player in their first team at 16 years, 244 days), Dulwich Hamlet, Cheshunt, Enfield, St. Albans City, Stoke City, Hull City (on loan), Cardiff City (on loan) and Bury
Signed for Leyton Orient: 1st July 1995
O's Debut: at Mansfield Town, 19th August 1995
Honours: Winners medal, 1991 Autoglass Trophy with Stoke City
Most Memorable Match: Liverpool v Stoke City, Littlewoods Cup, 1991/92. I scored the equalising goal

1st OCTOBER
1996

From the Leyton Orient programme, 1996

Man of the Match award at Leyton Orient, 1995

Scoring for Stoke against Bolton, 1992

Vilken avslutning i avslutningen! I sin sista match i Umeå (för alltid?) avgjorde Tony Kelly derbyt mot Umeå FC – i slutminuten! Inte undra på att lagkompisarna höjer honom till skyarna.
(Foto: MIKAEL LUNDGREN)

Kelly hyllas — en hjälte som gör skäl för namnet

Scoring the winning goal in my last match for Gimonäs,
against Umea in a Swedish derby

Wembley winners, 1991

The birth of my daughter Savanna, August 27 1997

With Savanna

Celebrating my equaliser against Liverpool at Anfield

With Abby (centre) and Mel (right) at the PFA Annual Football Awards

Going on to the pitch to do the half-time raffle as guest of honour when Stoke were playing Newcastle United in 2009

With prominent Stoke fan Nick Hancock when I was guest of honour at Stoke City, 2009

Me and Mel on his wedding day

In my Wembley winners' shirt

CHAPTER 5

Soccer Swedish style

My arrival in Sweden in April 1989 gave me an opportunity to put my name in the shop window as it were, not only in terms of the Swedish clubs but English ones too. My Director, John Mitchell, an ex-Fulham striker who had played in the same side as George Best in the 1970s, told me that if I did well it would soon filter through to the non-league circuit back in England, and this would alert English professional clubs to my progress.

It was a lucrative time for professional and non-league players coming to play in Sweden. Players like Vinnie Jones (now a famous Hollywood actor of course) and Dennis Wise had already made names for themselves before my arrival, not to mention ex-England striker Teddy Sheringham and others who followed.

I did have my concerns about the climate in Sweden - after all, it was never going to be the Caribbean – although I was told the summers were warm enough, so that was something to look forward to. It's not every day you get the chance to play football in a foreign country, so I just embraced the opportunity that had been presented to me, recognising the added bonus that I hoped to be able to keep my 'evil demon', gambling, at bay – for a few months at least.

All arrangements were in place and finally the big day came when I boarded a plane for Stockholm, where I was to meet my manager, Anders Johansson, at the airport. The uncertainty of stepping into the unknown made me curious and rather nervous, but I couldn't help but feel excited at the prospect of the new life ahead of me.

The lure of the krona was big back then as players knew they could either go on loan or secure long permanent deals, because the Swedes loved English soccer, not to mention the fact that English players were paid tax free. I was actually quite fortunate when I signed for Gimonäs CK as their neighbours and fiercest rivals, Umea FC, had just signed Lenny Dennis, a lad I had known well back in London. So at least I had someone I could hang with. That helped me to settle down and made my new life more comfortable. Lenny, like myself, was a striker and he was also trying to earn a pro contract in England, so we were both on a mission and would quickly become popular figures around the town of Umea.

Umea is a smallish town in the north of Sweden about two hours' drive from Stockholm. I found the people there to be very friendly and polite. I don't know whether that was because I was an English-speaking footballer but I'd like to think that they were just genuinely decent people.

The clearest memory I have of the town is the cleanliness. The streets were spotless, as it was against the law to drop litter, and it was enforced. When I think of the filthy streets of London and all the rubbish carelessly scattered around, the Swedish respect for their environment is all too clear.

After being picked up from the airport by Anders, I was taken to the Gimonäs stadium to be shown my new surroundings. Remember this was a second division club, and not a particularly wealthy one. Clubs such as Gothenburg and Malmö were the big players in Swedish football at that time and they played in the First Division, also known as the Allsvenska (All Sweden). At the back of my mind, I suppose I was hoping that a good season with Gimonäs might bring me to the attention of the Gothenburgs and Malmös of this world.

Anders was an articulate, sharp-dressing smooth type of guy, but he was not to be mistaken for a softie – he was far from that, as you would soon find out if you got on the wrong side of him. Anders spoke clear and fluent English and I sensed that he had a great knowledge and understanding of the game, both in

Sweden and England. He was well respected as a coach in his own country.

His coaching skills would be of great benefit to me as I was now training full-time on a daily basis, and the experience I would gain and the advice he gave me would help me to become a better player and ultimately to achieve my dream.

On arrival at the stadium I was a greeted by club staff and a few members of the local press. I must admit that I felt a bit of a celebrity – after all, here I was in a foreign country, a complete unknown, and the press wanted my picture already!

After a bit of chat and a few photos it was off to my new pad, a one-bedroom ground-floor flat which was only two minutes from the stadium. Although it wasn't quite a penthouse suite at the Hilton, it was clean, presentable and had all mod cons, which was fine by me. The management had even had the kindness to fill my cupboards with various kinds of food, which was a nice surprise.

Next it was back to the club for a chat and a coffee in the restaurant. I was very impressed by the generous treatment I was being given. I suppose the management felt they had to keep me sweet, but I felt they were going that extra mile to make sure I was comfortably settled in as well. It was a whole new experience for me to be in another culture in another country, but one I was already beginning to enjoy. I was also determined to make a success of it.

The one thing that did cause me a slight problem and would take a bit of getting used to was driving on the 'wrong' side of the road. The first time I drove off in the red Volvo the club gave me was a scary moment, as my trip was nearly over before it got started. As I pulled out of the little cul de sac by my flat to approach the main road, my mind was racing and I was desperately trying to keep a clear head and very conscious of the important of not making a wrong move. Sometimes when you try to be too careful you make a mistake – like when you are one against one with your keeper and you think too much about what you are doing. I must have looked left and right about twenty times, yet when I pulled out I still nearly hit an oncoming car head on! My heart pounded as I screeched desperately across to the other side. But as time went on I got used to the roads, as well as the weird sight of cars driving in daylight with their lights on.

Gimonäs was a well-run club with good discipline and excellent training facilities, and they were sponsored by Puma so I managed to amass a large collection of Puma gear – boots, trainers, tracksuits, even watches, all free of charge.

Being the equivalent of 'Football Conference' in England in terms of the standard of football in the Second Division and size of support, Gimonäs would only expect about a thousand supporters. As it was a nice tight compact stadium there a great atmosphere, especially on 'Derby Day' when Umea were in town. Such was the popularity of football in Sweden that most clubs also had a women's team, and Gimonäs was no exception. The women's team players would regularly watch the men and vice versa. It was obvious that some of these young and attractive female players also had their favourite men, so to speak. At home matches I would be grinning from ear to ear as I listened to the female fans screaming 'Go on Tony!' in their sexy Swedish accents. Naturally there was a lot of temptation to stray, and I couldn't help giving in to it sometimes, but I was happy in my relationship with Sandra so it was the football I focused on – most of the time, anyway!

I quickly settled in with my new team-mates and we agreed that we would all try to learn some Swedish, a scary thought, but I'm pleased to say I got on top of the language quite well. I would teach them certain English words and they would teach me Swedish ones. Needless to say the words they most wanted to learn were the unprintable ones!

There was a warm and friendly atmosphere in the dressing room and I felt that my presence seemed to help create a certain camaraderie and team spirit, which could only benefit us as a team and make us stronger.

The first few weeks were tough, as the weather wasn't great, in fact there was still snow on the ground and it was cold enough for us to wear our track suits and gloves in training. I had been warned of the cold before I arrived, so at least it did not come as a shock –

in fact I had been expecting more severe weather, so I was pleasantly surprised.

I started the season well, scoring on my debut, and quickly established an understanding of how the team played. It was pure football. Anders encouraged us to 'pass and move', which suited me, as my touch was good and my pace would be a great asset in the games to come.

One similarity between Swedish footballers and English players was that both enjoyed a drink – or ten! The Swedes liked to emulate the English drinking culture, either in the afternoons after training or down the local night club where they went to get smashed. However I found the Swedes to be generally a very friendly and placid people, and you were not likely to witness guys beating one another to a pulp after a few bevvies or see any of the violent behaviour you get in the UK.

Anders would often pop over to the flat for a chat, just to see how I was and make sure everything was OK. He managed to sort out a bank account for me so I could save some of my well-earned krona. This was something I had not been too good at in England because of my evil gambling addiction.

I did wonder if I would find an outlet for my bad habit in Sweden - there didn't seem to be any bookies around, fortunately - and sure enough it wasn't too long before one presented itself. I discreetly asked Mikhel, one of the lads, if anyone was into gambling, and I learned that some of them went on regular day trips to the 'races'. I had no idea what the 'races' were, but I imagined they were something like the horse-racing meetings we had in the UK. How wrong I was!

My first outing to the Swedish races was memorable, not to mention baffling, as it was nothing like what I had expected. I drew up with my new Swedish pals at a big venue which was more like a football stadium than a racetrack. As we walked into the main stand to take our seats, I looked down on the course to see that it was some sort of dirt track. When I saw what was happening I began to laugh hysterically. This was not horse racing in the conventional sense – there were horses, but they were harnessed to some kind of cart, and the jockeys were riding in the carts! I was baffled, as I couldn't work out what on earth was going on. The boys explained what it was all about, but I didn't really get it. All I really wanted to do was place a bet.

I splashed out a few krona on some horses with strange names and actually had a few winners – beginner's luck no doubt. Apart from being unable to comprehend the Swedish approach to racing, I did have a great time, and not surprisingly the boys and I were a bit the worse for wear at the end of the evening. We went on to attend quite a few more meetings after that, and of course the betting bug bit me all over again.

Soon after this I had a pleasant surprise – as I continued to flourish on the football field, I learned that big brother Errington was coming to join me at

Gimonäs. He had left his club, and I gave him a glowing reference to help him sign up with my club for the remaining months of the season. I was excited at the prospect of his arrival as I knew that Lenny, a team-mate called Junior and I would soon be causing havoc in more ways than one.

My girlfriend Sandra was coping with our long-distance relationship quite well and was busy with her work as a travel agent in London. I was in regular contact with Mel and some of our friends in London, but I didn't miss London life much – far from it in fact, as I had everything I needed in Sweden and was warming to the people and the culture. The Swedes liked to throw dinner parties, sometimes in the evening, sometimes in the afternoon. I enjoyed these as they were a nice way to get to know new people and brush up on my Swedish. By now Errington was fluent, and that helped in the bars and shops, although most of the Swedes spoke good English.

The 'London Brothers', as Errington and I were affectionately known, became a long-term fixture in this quaint little town. Errington brought his 1.4 litre burgundy Escort over, which he had bought from our sister. You can imagine the looks we got when we pulled up outside the local clubs – two black English guys in a right-hand drive car with UK plates. The locals were genuinely intrigued to find out what we were doing in their little town. They soon found out, as we were regularly featured on the sports pages of the local rag for our footballing exploits.

This was a magical time in my career, as I had my big brother with me and I was living like a celebrity in a foreign country which I was getting to be very fond of. Although black faces were scarce in Sweden and Errington and I were the only black players in the squad, there was no racism to worry about, in fact our team-mates and fans embraced us like royalty, which was great. I think it was a bit of a coup for Anders to get English players over to play for Gimonäs. Most people would be aware of the expense involved, but in return for his outlay we were making a big impact on the team's success. Gimonäs was riding high in the top three of the Swedish Second Division and the team was buzzing. In previous seasons the fans hadn't really had much to cheer about, so they were enjoying the taste of success.

I really did feel like a superstar as I swaggered around the night clubs with my wad of krona and not a care in the world. My favourite haunt was Fat Sam's Night Spot, the local night club, where the locals would get completely off their heads. The Swedes did love a drink, and it was funny watching them get into such a state as they downed pint after pint and sang their heads off.

Our status in the team attracted a lot of hangers-on. Not surprisingly, I didn't usually have to touch my 'wad' when I entered Fat Sam's. I would be bombarded with offers of drinks as well as questions and comments. Flattering as it was, it did get a little annoying, as I would often be itching to get away from the bar and throw a few shapes on the dance floor – I still loved my dancing. It was no surprise that the most questions came from the local ladies, and let's be honest, these blonde beauties were definitely premier league!

There was much banter and fun and games, but it was all in good taste and I did make some genuine female friends. Errington, being 'single', was like a dog on heat, and in Fat Sam's he was able to take his pick. Women would fall over themselves to mingle with us football celebs – I suppose in such a quiet, sleepy town in the middle of nowhere it was the most excitement they had seen in years.

One thing that was definitely not premier league was the Swedish dress sense. I mean, wearing your jeans halfway up your angles to show white socks is not a good look! Luscious as they were, the Swedish beauties could not match the London girls in the style stakes.

As I continued to work on my game and score more goals, I was soon aware that my contract was half way through and I was beginning to wonder if I would be able to stay in Sweden, such was the influence this lovely country was having on me. There was a mid-season break in July, with fixtures resuming in August, and as July approached I was really looking forward to my beloved Sandra coming over and spending some quality time with her and show her the sights. She arranged a two-week visit, which wasn't as long as I would have liked, but we had a good time, going out for meals and meeting my new friends. I did managed to get her to stay long enough to see me play at the end of her stay.

In August it was back to the grind of full-time training, to focus on my game and to make sure I made a good impression on whoever might be watching. My gambling had been temporarily kicked into touch, not because I had lost my appetite for it but because there were no bookies around to satisfy my urge.

Back home in England, I heard some interesting news from Bernard, my chairman at St Albans. My successes with Gimonäs had got back to some of the professional clubs and two in particular were making enquiries about my availability. What's more, they were both First Division clubs - Watford and Southampton! You can imagine my excitement. Although nothing was set in stone, Bernard did advise me that if I continued to progress there would be a definite choice of trials when I returned to St Albans.

I immediately told my family back in England the news, as I couldn't contain my excitement. Mel was pleased for me and encouraged me to keep up the good work. He was now well settled and happy with his life and very content in his relationship with Jacquie – in fact I could hear wedding bells ringing there.

Although Sweden is known for its snow and ice, they do have a summer there and I enjoyed a few wicked days on the beach with Lenny, Errington and Junior, banging out tunes from our ghetto blaster as we ran the rule over the local beach babes. I have never seen so many attractive, sexy women in one place in my life – it was a sight to behold. They must have felt a little intimidated with four pairs of bulging eyes undressing them!

Sadly my time in Sweden was coming to an end. I did have discussions with Anders about the possibility of staying on and the club sorting out a deal with St Albans, but it wasn't to be, as my contract clearly stated that the arrangement was for one season only, and St Albans wanted me back so that they could sell me on to another English club when the time came to raise funds. So I returned reluctantly at the end of the Swedish season, but in hopes that I might have a new break to look forward to.

Ironically my last fixture with Gimonäs was to be against our local rivals Umea FC, and what a game it was. As we arrived at the Umea ground just across town it was immediately obvious that the game had generated massive interest in the local community, as an hour before kick-off the stadium was already nearly full. As soon as I arrived I was swamped by autograph hunters and well-wishers, as it was now common knowledge that this was to be my swansong. I was excited, but there was also a touch of sadness, for I knew I would not see these wonderful supporters again. I had to wrestle with my mixed emotions as best I could.

With the score at 1-1 and the game at stalemate, it seemed the teams would be happy to settle for a draw and a share of 'bragging rights', but what happened next changed all that. As we entered the last minute of the match my good friend and team-mate Erik Bystrom scampered down the left wing. I reached the box and had the sudden feeling that this was a moment that had been written in the stars for me. Erik whipped a cross past the face of the goal into the six-yard box and I found myself perfectly positioned to slip the ball home, to the delight of our fans and my team-mates, with just seconds to go to the whistle.

We all went wild with joy and my team-mates hoisted me aloft, making sure I understood how much this meant to them. That image of me held high with my finger pointing a Number One will stay with me for ever. Fortunately the local paper's photographer captured that moment and printed it in the next day's edition. I kept the cutting and treasure it to this day.

So I managed to leave Gimonäs on a high, even a bit of a hero. I suppose it was fitting that I was able to end my wonderful time in Sweden in such a dramatic way, as my life was always full of drama and would continue that way; I didn't know it, but there were many more twists and turns in store for me.

Saying goodbye to my Swedish team-mates was one of the hardest things I have ever had to do, such was the bond we had built over those seven marvellous months. Still, it was just another chapter in my roller-coaster ride, and I now had to focus on trying to drive my career forward back home in England.

CHAPTER 6

Triumph and disaster on and off the pitch

It was with mixed feelings that I returned to England in November 1989. On the one hand I was happy to be seeing my loved ones again, especially Sandra, but on the other I knew how much I would miss what I had left behind. It was however time to move onwards and upwards in pursuit of my main goal, and focus on the future.

On my return I rejoined St Albans City as part of the deal that had taken me to Sweden, and it was great to catch up with the lads and talk about my experiences in Sweden. Fortunately my job at Eastern Electricity had been kept open, and I was able to continue full-time employment there. Getting by on my St Albans wages alone would have been very tough.

Unfortunately my family and Sandra were not the only ones I was looking forward to seeing again. I was also feeling an urgent need to become reacquainted with a certain Mr Coral and a certain Mr William Hill!

I'm afraid that the minute I got back to the UK the gambling bug struck again. Not that it had ever really left me – I just hadn't had much opportunity to indulge it. I couldn't wait to step inside the familiar surroundings of the bookie's once again. Coral's in Waltham Cross was just up the road from my work, so it was all too convenient. I was soon spending most of my lunchtimes here feeding my 'four-legged friends'.

I remember the first time I walked into Coral's on my return from Sweden. I immediately caught the familiar smell of cigarette smoke, and of course there were all my old pals lined up, waiting for the results and hoping for a big payday. My pockets were bulging, thanks to my stint in Sweden – I was armed and dangerous, to me that is. Whether I won or lost that first afternoon I don't remember, but I do know I immediately slipped back into my old habits. The fact that all the shops now had the SIS real-time information system installed added to the excitement and the pleasure, except of course that it also made it easier to see my money disappearing before my eyes!

My hunger for the buzz of placing a bet was obvious to all who were close to me. I did ask myself what I was thinking of giving in again to my evil habit, with a promising career, my girlfriend, my family and my friends to think about. However gamblers, like alcoholics, always want more. I had found that gambling was like a drug. You reach a point where you become dependent on it, and after that it starts to control you rather than the other way round. I found that although I would keep losing money betting on the horses and the football coupons, I still longed for the buzz of a win, and there lies the problem. Once you have experienced that buzz you always want it again, and you always believe in your luck – however many times you lose, you convince yourself you are going to win next time. Your fortunes can go up and down like a yo-yo, but in the end, as we all know, the bookies always come out on top.

The sad thing for me at this point in my life was that my habit was starting to have a bad influence on the people in my life. I kept being told "Don't lose what you haven't got" and "Keep to your limit", but of course I carried on regardless. There should have been alarm bells ringing, as the more I gambled the bigger the effect on my behaviour and the worse my mood swings. A 'bad day at the office' as they call it will only ensure you take your anger home with you, and it soon began to affect my relationship with Sandra.

How I itched to get my hands on the little red pens in the bookie's shop on dinner breaks from work. I would find the nearest bookies and start once again to indulge in my favourite pastime. Sandra had left her job at Ladbrokes, so she could no longer keep an eye on me from behind the counter there while I 'fed the horses', which made me even more vulnerable. I was digging myself a deeper and deeper hole, one which I would struggle to climb out of. Somehow I still did not feel I was an addict, even though I was gambling regularly and paying the price in more ways than one.

Mel was also gambling in a big way – being identical twins, naturally we did the same things. And he did have some big wins. I remember him phoning me one day and telling me to get round his pad sharpish. I knew from the tone of his voice that something exciting had happened, so I bombed down to the flat in Tottenham which he shared with his fiancée Jacquie. Our pal Jimmy was there when I arrived – he had obviously been summoned as well. Mel ushered us into the bedroom and said "Happy days, boys, I've had a bit of a win." With that he flipped open his black leather briefcase. It was stuffed with bundles of five and ten-pound notes. I couldn't believe my eyes. Mel had certainly had 'a good day at the office' and was understandably grinning from ear to ear. He had placed a 'Lucky 31' bet – five out of five winners at Royal Ascot – and won £1500. There is usually one horse that lets you down when you do an accumulator, but it all came good for Mel that day. Not a life-changing fortune perhaps, but back in 1989, it was a lot of money. We celebrated late into the night, and Mel splashed out £800 on a Ford Orion and put down a deposit on a flat.

So you see we both had the bug. After Mel's win I was even more determined to hit the jackpot myself as soon as possible, so that event did me no favours.

After a couple of trips to Coventry to see our friends BJ, Terry, Mark, Marie and the rest as well as my brothers, it was time to knuckle down and get my head in gear ready for the final six months of the season. Mum and Dad had now sold the family home back in Coventry and rented a place in High Wycombe, a sign of the times I suppose and the way people were coping financially. We had quite a few family and friends there. They soon settled down there, found jobs and began to get straight again, though getting back into the housing market in such an expensive area was out of the question. Dad was working in a furniture factory, while Mum returned to her own area of expertise, the fabrics business. Mel and I visited them there regularly, as did all of us. Meanwhile my sister Patricia had achieved her goal by becoming a full-time teacher in London.

I soon slotted back into my normal routine of scoring goals for St Albans, and the profile I had built for myself in Sweden was starting to get me noticed. It was my success in Sweden and my rapid progress on my return that would alert the 'big boys' of the football world on the soccer grapevine. I wasn't surprised to be summoned once again to the Chairman's office after training one night for one of those little chats. As you can imagine, my heart was pounding with anticipation as I sat in the big armchair facing his desk.

Bernard asked me if I would be interested in going for a week's trial with Southampton FC – a First Division side! I replied without hesitation that I most definitely would. He made it clear that no fees had been agreed, as this was only a trial. It would be up to me to prove I was worth a professional contract.

The trial would run from Monday to Friday with a reserve team game on the Wednesday, and I was promised a decision at the end of the week. As I left the ground and sped down the M25 in my BMW, my heart was pounding. I knew this was my big chance.

Sandra had my favourite spaghetti bolognese on the table when I returned home and she could see the excitement on my face. I told her the news and could see how pleased she was for me. She was always right behind me in my drive to get to the top.

There were a few sleepless nights leading up to the big day, as it dawned on me just how massive an opportunity this was. At that time the 'Saints' were riding high, blessed with such talents as Alan Shearer and Matt Le Tissier, who was voted PFA Young Player of the Year the following year, 1990, and went on to play for England eight times. Jumping from non-league football to the First Division with players like Matt and Alan around was a scary thought, but such was my desire to get up there with them that I couldn't wait to be given my chance.

On the day, I arrived at the Dell to find an army of flash motors in the players' car park. There were BMWs, Mercs and an assortment of sports cars, so my old BMW looked a little lost in that company!

I managed to get lost wandering through the many corridors and offices before eventually finding reception and sitting down to wait nervously for the manager, Chris Nicholl, to come out to meet me. After what seemed like an eternity a door opened and Chris appeared – a six-foot mountain of man and quite an intimidating figure. He welcomed me to the club with a handshake that nearly broke my fingers, then whisked me off to meet the rest of the squad.

At this point I must admit that I felt out of my depth. The sheer size of the stadium and its surroundings really brought it home to me that I was on the edge of the big time. I shook hands with Alan Shearer, Matt Le Tissier, Tim Flowers and several other star names I can't recall. It was such an honour and privilege to be in the company of top First Division players – after all, this was what I had been striving for all my footballing life.

The training was something else. If I had thought I was fit, the sessions at Southampton quickly brought it home to me that I was a long way from this standard. I did struggle a little on the stamina work we did, but to my pleasant surprise I actually came second in the sprints, so at least my pace would help me in what was to come.

After two days of training and bonding with the lads, it was time for my first big test – a reserve team match against Oxford United at the Manor ground. The reserve team consisted of a mixture of young pros (18-19 years old) and some senior players. I was really impressed by the technique of the pros, who would be pinging balls thirty or forty yards with frightening accuracy. Their 'first touch' was instant, so I suppose I felt a little inferior, but I did have my pace to help me.

The game itself was nothing to shout about, but I acquitted myself well. Although I was now playing with pros and against pros, I definitely didn't feel out of place. My speed gave the Oxford defence some problems, and after the game the other lads gave me plenty of compliments about my performance, as did the reserve team manager. So I now knew that I was at least up to reserve team standard, and that really pleased me.

The rest of the week went very well and I was able to hold my own in the company of the established professionals. Finally Friday came and it was time for Chris Nicholl to make his decision. I can't put into words what it would have meant to me if they had offered me a contract. It would also have taken me into the stratosphere, earnings wise.

Chris sat down behind his enormous desk and began to tell me how pleased he had been with my performance through the week. However, impressed as he was, he said there was a problem with the transfer fee St Albans was asking. It was way too high for a player who was unproven at professional level in England, so he could not offer me a contract unless my club dropped their price.

As he went on to explain the logic behind this, every word hit me like a dagger – I had wanted this so much.

I could see his argument and thought he was being perfectly reasonable, but it didn't make the disappointment any easier to bear.

Southampton were willing to pay £40,000 for me, a figure which would have been a non-league record transfer fee at that time. Yet unbelievably, St Albans was asking for £100,000! It was a ridiculous figure, and we both knew it.

I left the Dell shattered and disillusioned, but my devastation quickly turned to anger. My thoughts turned to Bernard Tominey and the realisation that my club's greed was stopping me from achieving my ambition. I was going to have some strong words for Bernard on my return to St Albans.

Sandra was upset for me, but she encouraged me to look on the bright side and not to consider giving up, as did my brothers and my mum and dad. After a depressing weekend I couldn't wait to confront the St Albans bosses and find out just why they had put such a big price tag on my head.

As I got dressed after the next Tuesday night training session down at Clarence Park, I steeled myself for my showdown with Bernard. I knew it would not be pleasant, and it wasn't. Having had my dream shattered by the club's greed, I was in no mood for patsying around, and I let him have it with both barrels.

He listened patiently. "Listen Tony" he bleated. "I can't let you go to Southampton for less than £100,000. They are a First Division Club, they can afford it. They've got buckets of money."

I'm afraid I just flipped. "This is bollocks!" I raged. "You know very well that £100k is way too much for a non-league player. You're out of order and you know you are. I'm not standing for it!"

But Bernard would not budge. I stormed out of his office with my head spinning, feeling even more confused than when I had gone in. I took ten minutes to calm down, then went back to his office. "That's it, I'm going on strike" I said. It was a bold threat, but I meant it. At that moment I felt I never wanted to play for them again.

In the end, after a couple of weeks off and a meeting to clear the air with Bernard and John Mitchell, Club Director, we came to an amicable agreement. They agreed that I was an asset to the club and that they valued me as a player. In return for a small pay rise, I agreed to play on, on the understanding that they would let me go for a £40,000 fee to any club that wanted me as long as it wasn't in the First Division.

With my name now circulating the non-league scene, interest was growing, and next in line was Watford FC. A special friendly match was arranged for me against a Watford side consisting of triallists, first-team players and reserves. Unfortunately I tried a little too hard, and although I scored in the first half I wound up limping off the pitch with a self-inflicted ankle injury, so my proposed move to Watford had to be put on hold.

Once I had recovered from my injury, I continued to develop, but I was now beginning to get more and more frustrated as still no firm bids had come in for my services. I was beginning to wonder just what I had to do to get the break I so desperately wanted. It was now 1990 and I was 23 years old – two years older than Matt Le Tissier and four years older than Alan Shearer. Time was already beginning to run out if I was to make it to the top in professional football.

I envied the wave of black footballers who were now flourishing in the game. Times had clearly changed since the 1970s and 80s as far as racism was concerned and it was good to see, although I wished I could join the revolution too, as it were. It was however obvious that pace was becoming a more important part of the game as we moved into the 90s, and scouts and managers were on the lookout for players who could show that extra turn of speed, so that was one thing in my favour.

Errington, Abby and Mel were all playing soccer at various levels and we would chat regularly about how our respective teams were getting on, and who had scored and who hadn't. It was good brotherly banter which reflected what an important part soccer was in all our lives, and would continue to be for years to come.

Not a week would go by now without my name being splashed across the sports pages of the *St Albans Gazette*. The goals were coming regularly, and such was the publicity I was now getting that I felt sure my time was near and that the big offer I craved was getting nearer. My intuition proved correct, as one day I got a phone call from my manager at St Albans to say that

Stoke City were interested, and would be coming along to our next match to take a look at me. I was excited at this news, but after what had happened with previous opportunities I was also cautious. I did want to have to deal with another false dawn.

Our next game was against Stevenage on a wet and windy Tuesday night at their ground. I remember the details very clearly. I was freaked out to think I was going to be watched by none other than Alan Ball, their manager, England international and a hero of the 1966 World Cup winning team, of which he had been the youngest member. Alan was known for his great skill as well as his incredible energy and determination, and I just hoped he would see something in me that would catch his eye. He had been promoted to manager the previous year (1989) after the dismissal of Mick Mills, and had got rid of many of the players, believing they were not up to standard. I was one of Alan's new intake, along with Tony Ellis, Lee Sandford, Dave Kevan, Paul Barnes and Noel Blake.

As the night of the match came I refused to allow myself to get nervous. In fact I remember being fairly relaxed, and it showed in the game, as I managed to put in an excellent performance, although it would have been even better if I had scored. We won the match 3-1 and my strike partner, Lance Pedlar, scored a hat trick. I suppose that could have created a danger that they would take on Lance instead of me, but I didn't worry about that as I had played well enough to feel confident.

After the game Bernard told me someone from Stoke would be calling the next day. The call duly came from Graham Paddon (ex West Ham and Norwich) who was the assistant manager at the time. He asked me if I was interested in going to Stoke for a trial.

My heart sank. I was looking for a contract, not another trial. I replied by explaining what had happened with Southampton and told him I was not prepared to go on any more trials.

I think Graham was a little shocked. Here I was turning down the opportunity to do a trial for Stoke City, a big Second Division club rich in history and with a stadium to match. Who did I think I was?

But I stood my ground, and Graham's attempts at persuasion fell on deaf ears. In the end he said he would have a word with the 'gaffer' (Alan Ball) and get back to me.

I didn't have to wait long. Within fifteen minutes Alan called me.

"OK Tony, we'll give you a two and a half year contract, as long as I can agree a fee with your club" he said. I was ecstatic. Thank goodness I'd stood my ground.

Then I realised I would once again have to square the offer with my chairman. This time, fortunately, Bernard and his board saw sense and agreed to let me go for the £20,000 offered, with a further £20,000 to be paid after I had made 25 appearances. That was a good deal for St Albans, and of course it was a great deal for me.

We arranged for me to go down in a couple of days'

time to sort out the arrangements. Back home, I told Sandra the news and she was as thrilled as I was.

Back in the 1980s most footballers negotiated their own contracts - there weren't many agents around, certainly in non-league football. I had taken advice from John Mitchell, my director at St Albans, and from my brother Errington, so I had a fair idea what a good contract would look like.

I got the train up to Stoke from London and took a taxi to the ground, arriving around mid morning. Alan met me at the players and staff entrance and I was immediately star-struck by his presence, not to mention a little nervous. After all, this man was a legend, not just in England but all over the world. Sadly Alan passed away only 17 years later at the age of 61 from a heart attack. I will always remember him and I will be forever grateful for the opportunity he gave me.

Alan was the perfect example of a professional footballer, and he knew how to conduct himself on and off the pitch. He told me that on the day he had come to see me at the Stevenage match he had not even got out of his car – he had sat there in the car park and watched me with his wife! He said he had seen enough to know he was going to sign me, and that made me feel ten feet tall. Not only was he a very funny man, he was one hell of a guy.

As Alan showed me around the Victoria Ground he gave me some words of wisdom and made sure I realised where I had arrived and what it meant. Stoke was a massive club with a huge fan base and a magnificent stadium. Unfortunately they were struggling in the Second Division at the time, which was a crying shame considering the status and history of the club. Pictures of the great players of the past were mounted on the corridor walls, men such as Alan Hudson, Stanley Matthews and Gordon Banks. I knew I had finally arrived. All those cold Tuesday and Thursday nights training had paid dividends and I could at last say to my friends and family the words I had been longing to let them hear: "I am a professional footballer."

My contract was worth £600 a week, which would rise to £800 subject to a win bonus and appearance money. To my very pleasant surprise I was also offered a £10,000 signing on fee, which I hadn't been expecting, although I had been advised to ask for one. I remember having this odd feeling that it was just too good to be true. I had gone from a £150 a week job to a monster wage, coupled with a fat cheque to take to the bank. I was in dreamland! Life for me would now take on a whole new meaning and I would move into a different world.

So keen was the gaffer to get me settled as quickly as possible that he offered me six months' free accommodation in a hotel, which made me feel like royalty. The hotel staff would see to my every need, and they went out of their way to make sure I was comfortable. I wasn't used to such treatment. The six months was designed to give me time to look for a house in the town, so in that sense it worked well.

Unfortunately I was now getting deeper into my gambling habit. My first thought when I woke up each morning was not what I was going to eat for breakfast or what time I was going to the ground but where and when I would be placing my first bet, and how much I had in my wallet to put on the gee-gees or the roulette table. Betting was constantly going through my mind – which horse will it be? Coral's or Ladbrokes? Go for a winner or try a combination?

Unfortunately the bookies were all too close at hand. Ladbrokes was just a two-minute walk away from my hotel. I had gambling debts in London, so I would visit my local bookie in Stoke and keep 'chasing', which means trying to win back money you have lost – a very foolish strategy, but one all gambling addicts fall prey to. With so much more money to play with thanks to my 'golden handshake', it wouldn't take a genius to work out that I was now in dangerous waters.

As I settled into my hotel room in the city centre, I was looking forward to my first training session, although I was extremely nervous about it. I remember being given my own spot in the dressing room, the place where I would be changing on a daily basis.

Meeting the squad was quite a thrill. There were some big names among them, such as Noel Blake, Peter Fox, Mark Stein and Ashley Grimes. I was with the stars now. I wasn't overawed by them however; I just wanted to show them that I too was worthy of my place in the squad, and it seems I made an immediate impact. To my amazement Alan told me I would be starting that same Saturday in the biggest match of the season so far, the Potteries derby against our local rivals Port Vale FC. When he broke this news to me on the Friday morning it took a while to sink in. After all, I had been playing for St Albans only the week before. I was certainly being thrown in at the deep end. In fact I thought it was madness, but Alan had faith in me and was confident that I could handle the step up in class.

I was quickly on the blower to let my family know the good news that I was already about to make my professional debut. Unfortunately I couldn't get enough tickets for everyone – after all, I did have very big family! I did get a few complimentary tickets and bought some additional ones some myself, as I wanted this to be a day to cherish for everyone.

I found the lads easy to get on with and they helped me to settle in. I soon got used to the banter that went on in the dressing room, and found no one was safe from the jibes and jokes. When I began training I wondered if they would dig me out, as you had to be on the ball and mentally strong, otherwise you would get slaughtered.

With the gaffer cracking jokes and telling tales, the dressing room was where everything happened, and I mean everything. Fights, bollockings, boot throwing, tea throwing – you did not want to get on the wrong end of one of Alan's bollockings.

My big day was February 3 1990. I had just bought a brand new jet black Rover 216i Vanden Plas and I felt on top of the world as I left the hotel drive the short distance to Vale Park, Port Vale's stadium. As I cruised through the town, everywhere I looked I saw armies of supporters from both sides making their way to the ground, all sporting their team colours. The town was buzzing, and I could feel the atmosphere all around me. It was clear to me that this game was a very big deal for everyone.

I remember the nervous tension building inside me as I took the field in front of 23,000 spectators, a sell-out crowd. This really was the big time. I had arrived, and now it was up to me to stay on top to make sure I had many more days like this to experience. I knew my fitness would be tested, as I was now playing Second Division football.

The game flew by, and my clearest memory of that day is the sheer pace of the game. Sometimes it felt as if I was chasing shadows. It was fast and frenetic, and to be honest, when I was substituted after 70 minutes I was relieved. By that time I was completely fucked!

So – debut over, and now it was time to establish myself in my new team and make my family proud of me.

If only my gambling hadn't been getting in the way. In today's society, and more importantly in the football world, gambling is becoming a major issue. The high street bookies no longer rely for their trade on a few old codgers spending a couple of quid from their pensions.

There is a new breed of gambler, with all too many opportunities to indulge his obsession.

Back in the early 1990s there were no 'mega slot machines', online bookies or late night TV gambling. Now it's all changed, and as a result gambling is out of control. With professional footballers earning anything from £2000 to £100,000 a week, you would think they would have so much money they would not feel the need to gamble. But gambling is a disease, and once you catch the bug it is incredibly hard to get rid of it. How much you happen to earn does not come into it. More money simply means bigger stakes, bigger wins – and bigger losses.

You do get a massive adrenalin rush sitting in a cosy, warm bookie's shop shouting your horse home, whether you have bet a fiver or £100. Research shows that among the 92 Football League clubs there are on average three players on every team who are addicted to gambling, and to be frank I think it's probably more than that. At least there is more help available today.

It's the emotional highs that motivate you to carry on gambling. One afternoon at Ladbrokes I put £50 on a treble, made up of three even-money favourites, and had two winners up, so I was waiting for the third, which promised a £400 payout. I couldn't stand to wait around at the bookies in case I had lost my last £400, so I waited till I got home that night and checked the results on Teletext. To my joy this particular horse had done the business and I had won. My 'happy cells' kicked in and the next day I went on a bender with the lads.

Yet on other occasions, when I lost most of my money, I would be overcome by feelings of depression. I would suffer sleepless nights, sweating and tossing and turning trying to tell myself it was OK. There was one night when I was chilling out at home in Stoke when I suddenly started to feel dizzy. My legs seemed to have turned to jelly, and when I got up to go outside for some fresh air I found I could hardly breathe. I felt I was about to pass out. After what seemed an eternity but was probably only a minute or so, I staggered outside into the cold night air and stood there shaking and taking long deep breaths. At last I felt OK again. I just flopped on the doorstep, wondering what had hit me. It had been a panic attack of course, brought on by stress, worry and lack of sleep.

That's what gambling does to you – it takes you on a roller-coaster ride through all the emotions from exultation to total despair. Naturally this affected my game. When I had won, I would be on a high and play well, but when I would lost it would usually lead to a stinker on the pitch.

I was now deep in debt and my addiction was reaching new heights. On an away trip with Stoke they were running a 'card school' and of course I was soon a full member. Six or seven of us would sit round a table at the rear of the coach to play Three-Card Brag. This wasn't just a pleasant little diversion to while away the time – it was hardcore gambling with big money changing hands and IOUs being issued all the time. It wasn't unusual to lose £1000 in half an hour.

I was loving every minute of being a professional footballer and all the benefits that went with it, but in one match I got a taste of the nasty side of football which still tarnishes the game. One wet Tuesday night we were playing West Bromwich Albion at the Hawthorns and I soon discovered that I was a marked man. As I jumped for a ball from the keeper's goal kick, I suddenly found myself on the ground spitting blood and teeth. Craig Shakespeare's elbow had just smashed into my face. Until you get properly clued up on the pitch, you don't see these attacks coming. I have never felt such searing pain. It felt as though all my teeth had been ripped out with a pair of pliers.

After coming round, minus three of my teeth, I stupidly managed to persuade my physio that I was OK to continue. I can't believe I went on and finished that match. I must have been on another planet in the last 20 minutes. Shakespeare wasn't even booked.

After the match the doctor and the physios rushed me to an emergency dentist. Every time I look in the mirror I am reminded of that night by my two screwed-in false teeth. At 23 I was soon established in Stoke's first team and enjoying life in the fast lane. I would buy £300 suits and gold chains and sovereigns thinking I was making a statement about my success, but in truth all I was doing was presenting the image of a typical flash footballer with an ego to match. I was having one hell of a time, but when I look back at it now I see how my reckless ways were spiralling out of control without me realising it until it was too late.

Although my relationship with Sandra was still strong, it was strained by my escalating gambling activities and my roving eye. I found it hard to resist the temptations that kept being thrown my way. After all, I was in a world of fame and fortune and mixing with celebrities, going to house parties and champagne parties. I was having a really good time.

I remember a night out at the Spot Club in London's Covent Garden, a regular haunt for prominent footballers. I was with Mel, Abby and a few footballing friends. We had just been to the PFA awards at the Grosvenor Hotel in Hyde Park and were smashed by the time we arrived at the Spot Club. I hit the dance floor – and before very long I had stripped off my blazer, tie and shirt and was dancing topless. I must have looked like some maniac on crack, prancing around as if I owned the place. It wasn't as if I played for Manchester United!

As I went on chatting to a series of shapely, scantily-dressed female punters and downing bottle after bottle of Budweiser, I was approached by a serious-looking doorman, who told me to get my shirt back on or else. As I didn't fancy getting a kicking in front of the football celebs, I did as he said. My reputation in Stoke was certainly growing, but not for the right reasons. Drama was never too far away.

Sadly, all Alan Ball's efforts could not save us from the drop that year after a disappointing finish to the season, and we found ourselves down in Division 3. In the summer of 1991 ex-Manchester United and Scotland star Lou Macari took the reins. He brought a fresh spark to the club, and his fitness regime became legendary, as did his disciplined management. I had an instant rapport with Lou, who seemed to take to me, which was quite surprising considering he was well aware that I was a bit of a jack the lad.

I think my fitness and speed enabled me to stay in our new gaffer's sights, as he made it clear that fitness was critical - our long training sessions in the afternoons were evidence of that. There were no more 12.30 pm finishes and shooting down to the pool hall or the pub, or in my case to the betting shop. We would regularly train twice a day, something the lads were not used to, and believe me, we hated it. Although we moaned about it, as footballers do, it proved to be astute management by Lou as we began to make a strong push for promotion and soon had the Football League Trophy in our sights. I didn't mind the extra training, but I'm afraid I did mind not being able to spend my afternoons at the bookies'.

Around this time Lou signed an Australian player whose name I can't recall. We quickly became pals off the pitch, and I soon found out that he liked a bet as much as I did. It was this guy who first introduced me to The Casino in Stoke. The first time I went it was out of simple curiosity. I was intrigued by the amount of money you could win – a nice jackpot of a few thousand pounds could pay off my debts all in one go. And it stayed open till four in the morning – plenty of time to get rich!

I started with a little beginner's luck, winning a few hundred pounds on the roulette wheel. But it wasn't long before I lost it again, and of course I started chasing and wound up cleaned out again.

On one of my bad days at Ladbrokes I managed to chase and lose my whole week's wages, £800 by then, in one nightmare Friday afternoon. As I walked out of the bookies it suddenly hit me that I wouldn't be able to get to training next week – I was completely cleaned out. The shock of what I had just done suddenly hit me.

Needless to say I had a stinker of a match that Saturday, and it was at that point that I realised my addiction was affecting my performance on the pitch. I actually had to scrounge some loose change from my neighbour Gareth for food for the weekend.

Sometimes in life you have to swallow your pride and start being honest with yourself. I decided that when Monday morning came I would speak to Lou and put my cards on the table, if you'll forgive the pun. After I had poured out my problems I had a pleasant surprise. He seemed to understand what I was going through and allowed me to borrow £300 from petty cash, for which I was immensely grateful. He was a man I found I could talk to about personal matters, and I think he knew I had more to offer the club if he could help me through my troubles.

Under Lou's regime the players reached new heights

in a match which will ever be remembered by Stoke fans. It was a League Cup tie against Liverpool at Anfield on September 25 1991.

To play at Anfield in front of 35,000 Scousers would have been an experience in itself. But what happened to me will live long in the memory, and I still check out You Tube sometimes to remind myself that it really happened.

There were few tougher challenges in football than playing Liverpool at home when they could field a squad full of stars like as Bruce Grobbelaar, Dean Saunders, Mark Walters, Steve McMahon and Ian Rush. We knew there was virtually no chance of beating such a team on such an occasion, so we were relieved to find that as full time approached we were only 2-1 down – an honourable result.

But then events took an unexpected turn. With two minutes to go to the final whistle, as the Stokeites sang *Delilah* and the Kop got ready to celebrate yet another victory, my moment of opportunity suddenly arrived. I was put clean through the forward line and found myself alone and facing the formidable Grobbelaar.

Time stood. Still. Six thousand Stoke supporters held their breath, along with God knows how many of my family and friends, as I composed myself, drew back my right foot - and slotted the ball straight between the big man's legs.

Wild ecstasy followed. I shouted my joy to the Stoke fans behind the goal, and to this day I cannot put that feeling into words. I remember commentator Clive Tilsley saying 'You won't get a ticket for love nor money when these two teams meet again at the Victoria ground in a fortnight's time'.

Our 2-2 draw was the shock of the round, as of course Liverpool were in Division 1 and we were still in lowly Division 3. It proved what a fine side Lou was fielding at that time. I'm afraid I don't remember much about the party we had afterwards, except that I'm sure it was my best-ever night out in my time at Stoke. I do recall walking into Maxim's, the local nightclub, around midnight with my cousin Ray and my brothers and being mobbed, followed by chants of 'There's only one Tony Kelly' to the tune of *Guantanamera* belted out by around 50 Stoke fans as they proceeded to drink themselves into a happy oblivion. Needless to say I didn't buy a drink all night.

Such was the euphoria among Stoke fans at the scale of our achievement that the next day my phone was ringing off the hook. I stuttered and muttered my way through interviews with *Match* magazine, *Shoot* and the national press, but by that time all I wanted to do was get back in the sack and sleep! I felt like a big time celebrity, and of course I wanted the feeling to last forever.

The return leg at the Victoria ground two weeks later was a very different match. This time I was the villain instead of the hero. A packed house watched in horror as I slipped up and sent a back pass straight to the 'poacher supreme', Ian Rush, who immediately scored

– and our fate was sealed. My first-half mistake probably cost us the match. We were 2-0 at half-time and Lou was not a happy man. It was the only goal of the match. Football has a cruel way of kicking you in the bollocks, and I was always brought back down to earth in the end.

However the season continued in a positive way and by the turn of the year we were again eyeing a place at Wembley. It is every schoolboys' dream to play at Wembley of course – not the ground it has become today but the legendary 'Twin Towers' ground, or the 'home of football' as it is often referred to.

Off the pitch, I just didn't seem to be able to stay out of mischief at this time. My womanising ways almost got me the kicking of my life. Having become a 'face' in Stoke, I allowed my ego to get the better of me.

After a night out with Mel, Abby and my cousin Ray at my favourite nightspot, the Place, I was confronted by a black geezer as I stepped out into the street outside the club. I had no idea who he was, but he obviously knew me. Before I knew it we were surrounded by some angry-looking guys shouting 'Vale, Vale, Vale!' It seemed that this man had not only discovered I had been messing around with his woman - he was a Port Vale supporter!

Things didn't look too healthy. After a heated exchange I realised I had to get out of there, and quick. After a quick glance at Abby and Mel I took the hint and legged it. I never thought I would have to use my pace to save my skin in such a frightening situation. I looked over my shoulder to see the pack running after me. I was in such a panic that my legs buckled and I crashed to the pavement. I was wearing a new Boss suit and I remember thinking 'Shit, my suit's ruined'. What a ridiculous thing to worry about! But luckily I was able to get to my feet and escape into the night.

When I met up with Mel and Abby later I was amazed to hear that Ray had stayed behind and taken some of the baying mob on. To this day he still doesn't know why he did that. Except of course that he had had a skinful.

I stayed out of town for a few weeks after that as I was now a marked man, and it wasn't a nice feeling having to look over my shoulder every minute. Fortunately things soon died down and it wasn't too long before I was free to roam the streets and get up to no good again.

Meanwhile the gambling continued. I was blind to the level of debt I was now getting into. I was soon behind with all my bills, including my mortgage, but however bad things got I just couldn't shake off the urge to try for the 'big one' – a classic gambler's mentality.

I was now a regular at the casino and was spending many an afternoon there, more often than not crying into my beer by the end of it. Roulette was my game. The mistake all gamblers make of course is to ignore that wise saying 'Quit while you're ahead'. I would be on a winning streak with my numbers coming up and a pile of chips in front of me, but instead of calling it a day and taking my winnings home I would get greedy and try to go for more, forgetting that of course the house always wins in the end. Eventually I would lose all my winnings and leave with nothing – and trust me, that hurts.

My family did not appreciate how serious my habit was back then. In hindsight of course I wish I had sought help, but I'm afraid I just enjoyed going to the bookies' and the casino and filling out my football coupons too much, despite the repeated pain of losing.

The more I lost the more desperate I was for that life-changing win and the more convinced I was that one day it would come. Of course, it never did.

On a happier note, my career at Stoke continued to flourish. Incredibly we reached the Autoglass Trophy Final, to be played on May 16 1992 at Wembley Stadium. As the date of the match approached my boyhood dream of playing at Wembley looked like being shattered, as I strained my knee ligaments just a week before the final. I discussed the problem with Lou, who was very concerned that my injury could cost me an opportunity I might never have again - most pros go through their entire careers without ever having a chance to play at Wembley. He offered a solution – a cortisone injection. It would hurt, but that wasn't going to put me off it if it meant I could play on the hallowed turf. So I took his advice. For ten or fifteen seconds the pain was incredible, but it was well worth it as it made it possible for me to play that match.

Any team that reaches a major cup final is going to attract a lot of media attention, and we were no exception. We had fittings for new suits and interviews and even spent two days at a health farm in the lead-up to the big day. We were thoroughly pampered. The match was to be broadcast live on Sky, and I was chuffed that my friends and family back in Coventry would be able to watch it.

When the big day dawned, the city went cup final crazy. There was a terrific buzz all around the town, everyone had big smiles on their faces and you could see how the whole place was caught up in 'cup fever'. 50,000 'Stokies' were getting ready to descend on the town, and I couldn't wait to be part of it.

As we travelled down in our smart, upgraded coach, you won't be surprised to hear that as usual I was playing cards – but no money was changing hands on this journey. We had better things to think about.

My first memory of seeing a cup final on telly had been the West Ham–Fulham tie in 1975, and the phrase I remember was the 'Wembley Way'. I was about to experience my own Wembley Way.

At last the coach cruised down the real Wembley Way en route to the stadium entrance, and as I looked out of the window I began to shed tears of sheer joy and excitement at the massed crowds of fans. It was stunning to see that endless sea of red and white and all those people singing their heads off in our support.

Wembley is supposed to be a demanding pitch which saps players' strength and brings on cramp and fatigue, but I didn't feel any of that myself after warming up. I did feel nervous though. As the minutes ticked by towards kick-off I was gripped by tension, but the knowledge that my family were out there made me determined not to let them down, and not to let myself down.

The dreaded walk from the changing room through the tunnel at Wembley is an experience no footballer who has played there will ever forget, for one particular reason – the 'Wembley Roar'. As you approach the end of the tunnel you see the pitch and stands ahead of you, and as you emerge into the sunlight that roar hits you like an express train. It's deafening, terrifying and wonderful all at the same time. It was one hell of a proud moment as I gazed round at those 60,000 people. I really had got to the top and made it in pro football at last.

It was a hot day, and I remember thinking as I walked out on to the hallowed turf that I must not let anyone down. Millions of people were watching on Sky, and I really didn't want all those people to see me have a stinker.

The game started at a frantic pace and I remember getting chopped down on the right wing. On the TV, commentator 'Big Ron' Atkinson was saying 'They're going to try and use Tony Kelly's pace down this right side'. I took another knock on my ankle in the first half and was just praying I could run it off, as there was no way I was going to come off injured in front of my family and all my friends.

I struggled through to half time and fortunately the pain eased in the second half. I played OK, although not at my best, but at least I wasn't affected by that energy-sapping pitch, so I kept going for the full 90 minutes. The game stayed fairly even until the magic moment in the 65th minute when Vince Overson helped the ball into the Stockport box and Lee Sandford flicked it on beyond the static Stockport defence to our 'pocket rocket', Mark Stein. From 12 yards he volleyed an unstoppable shot into the roof of the net. That was the only goal of the match. 40,000 Stokies went wild, and Steiny's name was written into Stoke folklore for ever.

As the champagne flowed in the dressing room and the lads chatted about the game, I felt I couldn't wait to see Mum and Dad. I knew how proud Dad was of me – after all it was he who had started me out on this journey 14 years before as a skinny little nine-year-old at Coundon Cockerels.

I felt drained physically and mentally by the time I walked into the players' lounge, but I was so thrilled to see my family and Sandra. We chatted through the evening, and we must have had a few as I don't recall too much after that!

As the season drew to a close with my cup winner's medal sitting proudly on my mantelpiece I was pleased to be offered a fresh two-year contract. Lou Macari believed in me and knew how much more I still had to give – if only I could manage to sort my personal issues out, namely my gambling addiction. Sadly that demon still controlled me, and I'm afraid the £10,000 joining fee was only enough to clear a fraction of the debt I had already accumulated. It seems crazy, I know – there is no logical reason why someone earning a large salary would gamble it all away rather than putting it in the bank or investing it. But then there is nothing logical about gambling – it's an irrational, evil addiction. Why else would someone who has lost £1000 in a week put another £200 of borrowed money down on a horse in the vain hope of getting it back? But that's what gamblers do, all the time, sinking deeper and deeper into debt and despair. And then if you do win you imagine you have hit a winning streak and you put it all on another horse – with the inevitable result.

A bookie's shop can be the loneliest place in the world. After spending a whole afternoon chasing an imaginary jackpot I have all too often found myself sweating with fear over the prospect of another loss, pacing up and down and barely able to look at the screens. By the end of the afternoon the bins would be overflowing with crumpled scraps of paper, each one representing the shattered dream of a loser, and mine were right in there with them.

I remember losing out on a £4000 payout for a 'placepot' bet at York Races one afternoon. My horse had only to finish in the final three for me to win. The horse was the hot favourite – and then disaster struck. It was pipped into fourth place by a nose. I just could not believe it. Yet there are thousands of hard luck stories like this to be told in every betting shop.

You may have beginner's luck or hit a winning streak, but in the long term you can only lose. There is no such thing as a poor bookie. Remember, losing gamblers don't talk about their failures. For every story of a big win you hear – like a couple I have told in this book - there are hundreds of losers who had to slink home penniless after staking their shirts on one bet too many.

So my memories of my time at Stoke are filled with a mixture of happiness and sadness. Those wonderful highs of my goal at Anfield and that magical day at Wembley will stay with me forever. I will ever be grateful to the late Alan Ball and to Lou Macari, as they gave me something that can never be taken away, something I can cherish for ever. Looking back at the Stoke days, the womanising, the gambling, the street brawls, the bling, the wild spending and of course those wonderful moments on the pitch have left me with a rich store of memories. Unfortunately, they include too much evidence of those demons I could not conquer.

Extra time

As the 1993-4 season went on I found myself out of the side as often as not. My gambling addiction was at its height and I was suffering mentally, which coincided with a massive drop in form. Lou Macari could see I was a troubled soul and it was time for another move. I was invited to speak to Mike Walsh, the manager at Bury FC. Mike invited me to come and play with them against Wigan on loan the following Saturday. He had already agreed a transfer with Lou. So I took a chance; I couldn't help thinking that it would mean another of those fat cheques I kept needing.

Fortunately for me I scored on my debut with Bury, which helped me to secure a two-year contract with a £15,000 signing-on fee. I didn't know it at that time, but I would never again reach the dizzy heights of playing at championship level in front of big crowds.

Moving from Stoke City to Bury should have been a

warning sign that I must be doing something wrong. After all, I was still only 26 years old, supposedly the age where the average footballer reaches his peak. So why was I taking a backward step instead of a forward one?

Looking back, the simple reason was that I was not sufficiently dedicated to the job. Add to that my gambling addiction, and you can see that I was heading for failure.

It's sad to think that after all I had achieved as a teenager and my memorable moments at Stoke, not to mention my success in Sweden, I had now begun a bumpy but unstoppable slide down the football ladder. I was still earning a good wage and doing the job I loved, but the reality was I had sold myself short, big time. My gambling and wild nights out at Stoke were coming back to haunt me.

The writing had been on the wall for several weeks by the time I left Stoke. Of course, my evil gambling demon was all too willing to help me waste that fifteen grand at the first opportunity.

Looking back, I will always cherish my memories of those years at Stoke. If I could turn back the clock I would try to arrange things so I could stay longer, but at the time I was willing to start a new beginning. I wanted to get my personal life, as well as my career, back on track.

Bury was a nice, well-run League 2 club with a wealthy chairman called Terry Robinson. In the office one day I was introduced to someone called Neville. In fact he was called Neville Neville! His sons were well known on the pitch as the Neville brothers, Gary and Phil.

As I set about finding my feet I moved into a rented house with a promising young player called Jimmy Mulligan, an unassuming Irish lad. I soon found that we had something in common – Jimmy liked a bet nearly as much as I did. We would chat during training about what time Kempton Races started or who we were going to back on the midweek football coupons. Gamblers are always looking for the next fix.

It must have been around this time that I got my first mobile phone. It was absurdly big and clumsy compared to today's phones and I must have looked as if I was carrying a brick, but I went around all day posing with it! Unfortunately using a mobile wasn't cheap in those early days and in the first month I ran up a £500 bill, and that was without the premium lines!

I was now a big fish in a small pond, having made my name at Stoke, as a bigger club. The other players called me TK and I swaggered around as if I was lord of the manor.

I might have been the king of the partygoers among the squad but I was definitely not the hardest – that honour belonged to an East End lad called Ronnie Mauge, who had joined the team from Fulham. Having both come from London we had something in common, and we soon struck up a friendship. Ronnie was quite a character. Though he stood only five feet eight, he was as hard as nails and didn't hesitate to show it. Some of the lads were scared of him, but not as scared as the opposing teams were.

Like me Ronnie loved a night out, so it wasn't long before we were both making our mark on Bury city centre, as well as Bolton. Our regular haunt was a very popular club called Benny's, which lay in a secluded spot at the end of a long dirt track. It was frequented by footballers from several clubs, including Preston, Bolton, Rochdale and Oldham as well as Manchester United and Manchester City. Right next to Benny's was Robson's Bar, owned by the former United and England player Bryan Robson. We would down a few there before moving across to Benny's to start causing our customary havoc. I'm afraid we acted like flash, arrogant, pretentious pricks – the worst side of the pro footballer.

Ronnie and I were friendly with another player, Roger Stanislaus, who was the opposite to Ronnie. He was a cool dude who had a calming influence on us - except when he was fully plastered himself!

Benny's was a fun place with a great vibe, not to mention some sexy women who made no secret of what they were looking for. Unfortunately I found out quite quickly how much trouble these manhunters could get you into. One night at Benny's I pulled a tasty bit of stuff and we were soon in a taxi on the way to her place. She assured me I was welcome to stay over, and she was making it pretty obvious she didn't mean just for a coffee and a chat.

When we got there her home turned out to be an

old Victorian house, well furnished and spotlessly clean and tidy. My new conquest led me upstairs, and I was full of anticipation of the delights in store. But as we romped on the bed half naked, I suddenly heard from the bottom of the stairs the unmistakeable sound of a key in the door. I asked the girl if she had heard it and she pooh-poohed my alarm. I don't know whether that was because she really hadn't heard it or she was just too keen to get on with the business in hand!

Before we could discuss it any further I heard the door open and boots thundering up the stairs. Now I knew I was in trouble. I pushed the girl off me and sprang to my feet, now down to my boxers. The bedroom door flew open to reveal a big, evil-looking black geezer, well-built and with fury in his eyes.

Now as a fit pro footballer and a fairly big guy myself I could manage in a tight corner, but just as I was preparing myself for his attack he rushed past me, grabbed the poor girl off the bed and kicked her down the stairs. I still felt in danger, but knew I had to step in and help her. He began to rain punches down on her and it was an awful thing to witness. My instinct began to kick in – I couldn't stand by and watch this guy beat his woman to a pulp. But as I went down the steps towards them, he turned to me again and pulled out a knife! It wasn't a little pen-knife either, but a big, shiny butcher's knife.

'Come any further and I'll fuckin' do ya!' he yelled. I froze. What to do now? Well I could have tried to tackle him in my bare feet and boxers, but I was young, life was good and I wanted to go on living it. It was bedroom window or Bury Mortuary, and the former seemed, on balance, the better option. So I legged it. Unfortunately I left half my belongings behind in my haste, but it was a small price to pay for freedom and safety.

Unfortunately I wasn't quite out of trouble yet. I jumped out of the window on to the roof of what I thought was a garage below, only to find it was just a wooden shed. I crashed straight through the boards. When I picked myself up I was covered in cuts and scratches and what clothing I had on was ripped. I must have looked quite a sight as I tried to flag down a cab at 3 am. Fortunately a good Samaritan took pity on me and gave me a lift, and I managed to get home in one piece, although I was a bit shell-shocked.

By now I suppose the penny should have dropped. My reckless lifestyle was threatening my health, my bank balance and on this occasion my life, but I carried on living as if there was no tomorrow, doing what I wanted to do when I wanted to do it, with no thought for the consequences. My gambling was reaching new extremes. I had become a regular at the Bolton casino, usually after a night out at the nearby Ritzy. I can't tell you how many times I left that place without the money for a cab home. It became quite normal to lose £500 on a roulette table in an hour. Yet always I would go back, chasing and chasing, oblivious to the depth of the hole I was digging for myself.

And the tragic thing is, for the gambling soccer player nothing has changed - except the amount of money that changes hands. What the answer is I have no idea, but it's imperative that something is done. Football clubs up and down the country need to realise how much trouble some of their players are getting into.

Understandably my relationship with Sandra had now become very uncertain, off as much as on. Much as I loved her, I just could not settle down in the way she was hoping. She was – and still is - a diamond of a woman who has been through everything with me, the highs and the lows, the triumphs and the disasters, and after being close for 26 years we still look back sometimes and think 'if only'.

Funnily enough, although my personal life was a mess, my football skills were flourishing at this stage. We managed to reach the semi-final play-off against Preston, and as the date of the tie approached I had flashbacks to a certain Wembley engagement. I don't know if I'm jinxed, but trouble and drama seem to follow me around. What was supposed to be a new highlight in my topsy-turvy career turned into a complete disaster. In front of a packed house at Gigg Lane I managed to exceed my own previous misdemeanours by getting myself sent off!

I started dancing around Ryan Kidd (the son of the famous ex-Manchester United and Manchester City striker Brian Kidd). I was throwing jabs as if I was in the boxing ring. God knows what was going through my head, but I completely lost the plot. I can't really blame the referee for showing me the red card.

The consequences of my little act of madness only came to light in the dressing room after the match. We managed to win the match, so my team would now be playing at Wembley – but they would be appearing without me. Being sent off meant an automatic three-game ban. I pleaded with the club and they tried to pull strings, to no avail. I just had to take it on the chin and suffer the consequences of my actions.

At the age of 27 I was still well capable of playing at Premiership level. I now went through a purple patch when I seemed to be scoring goals for fun. When we played Stockport County at Gigg Lane on a miserable Tuesday night, I scored two crackers, but then got hammered by their unforgiving left back and twisted my ankle ligaments. My goals gave us a 2-0 victory, and when I knocked on the door of the gaffer (Mike Walsh) after the match I saw a crowd of faces. One of them was Peter Reid, the ex-Everton and England player. 'Orl roight TK?' he said in his Scouse accent. 'You were fuckin' brilliant tonight, and I tell you what lad, you can go as far as you want to, it's up to you lad.'

I walked out of that office with a spring in my step and feeling ten feet tall, even though I was actually on crutches. But I should have heeded that 'It's up to you'.

In those two years at Bury, there was never a dull moment. Given my taste for the night life it was inevitable my party-crazy lifestyle would catch me out again before long, however. One evening, after a night out at Bolton Ritzy, I took one risk too many and drove home (with a leggy blonde passenger of course) after having drunk one too many. I knew my number was up when I saw the blue lights flashing in my rear view mirror. I couldn't blag my way out of this one, so it was goodbye to the blonde, goodbye to the car and hello to a locked cell for the night.

That brought an otherwise exciting and promising season to a sorry end. We lost the play-off 2-0, a bad blow for the club, and never recovered. My second season with Bury went by in a flash. I continued to perform well (on and off the pitch!) but as a team we never reached the heights of the 1993-94 season. I was just as well I had tasted Wembley glory with Stoke, but I still felt the pain as I sat on the bench watching our dream of promotion evaporating.

At the end of that season the chance came up to transfer to Leyton Orient. I could have stayed with Bury, but I was keen to take the opportunity to start a new life in the 'Big City' and see more of Mel and the rest of my family and friends.

The next defining moment in my life was meeting the man who was to become my agent and negotiated my new berth at Leyton Orient for me. Being sceptical about agents – I saw them as no more than sharks who were just after your money – I didn't see myself using their services. But on my return to London I met Peter Abdou. I don't remember how I met Peter, but by chance he happened to live near my long-suffering girlfriend Sandra. Or should I say ex-girlfriend, because at this time we were going through a separation, although we were still very close and very fond of each other.

The new supremo at Leyton Orient was Barry Hearn, the sports promoter who made a fortune from snooker and went on to work his magic with boxing, darts and football. He had just come in as chairman and invested in the club. He managed such household names as Steve Davis, Nigel Benn and Chris Eubank and was a very well-known name. So when I walked into his office with Peter in tow, I was hoping he would be able to stand up to Barry.

I need not have worried. They got to the point pretty quickly, as Barry was a straight-talking man who didn't mess about. 'I don't give signing-on fees, but you'll get a good wage' he said. The transfer from Bury was agreed at £40,000. True to his word we did get the wage we wanted, and the £7500 'relocation fee' was a nice added bonus. So Peter did well, though his request for a company car for me was turned down sharpish!

There was a real 'feelgood factor' at Orient, as I was in on the start of something of a revolution. Since Barry had bought the club he had added some much-appreciated glamour and glitz. Home matches were literally given the red carpet treatment – players would stride out on to the pitch over a crimson carpet while stirring music played. It was just like Hollywood! Each game attracted a new celebrity – boxers, snooker players, footballers, page 3 models all came along to help turn us into the Manchester United of Division 3. I was looking forward to the season ahead. The 'Os' looked to be going places.

When I moved back to London I discovered that I was at last living in a multiracial society. Relationships between blacks and whites were much more overt and much less tense. Times had changed, thank goodness. Having said that, I still found that although there were many more black players around and simple racism was less of a problem, there were still cliques in the dressing rooms. I have played for six clubs, and the players in all of them had the same tendency to form cliques. There would be the quiet ones in one corner, the 'brothers' (us blacks) in another, the 'party animals' in a third, and so on. In a multiracial society, surely people should be mixing freely. It bugged me that the managers seemed to encourage this divisiveness, for example by putting members of the same clique together when we were room-sharing on an away trip. Surely this is wrong – learning about each other's culture and background is a good thing, and educationally it can teach our younger players a great deal.

I'm pleased to say I quickly became a crowd favourite down at Brisbane Road and managed to score a few goals. My £7500 cheque enabled me to put down some money on a flat in Enfield, but I'm afraid a large chunk of it was spent at the 'office' – Ladbrokes of course. I moved in with Mel while waiting for the flat to be sorted, and it was right round the corner from the local bookie's. I would finish training at 1 pm and shoot off down to Ladbrokes to meet Mel and John. The three of us would spend most of our afternoons crying into our coffee, usually walking home without a bean between us.

Looking through my memorabilia the other day, I was amazed to find a betting slip with my handwriting on it from 1997. It said 'Kelly 1st goal scorer 12/1'. Can you believe I had started betting on myself? No wonder I was skint! I had no defence against my gambling demon, always persisting under the illusion that the jackpot was just around the corner.

My love of night life continued unabated after I moved back to London, and I now had some exciting new places to strut my stuff, such as Charlie Chan's and Epping Forest Country Club. These were the 'in' clubs for celebs and soccer players and you can imagine the kind of women they attracted – short skirts, high heels and low morals.

At the end of my first season with Orient, Mel, Abby and I attended the PFA Annual Players' Awards - once again. This was a night to remember. As we brothers and a few friends were partying the night away I was approached by an obvious wannabe WAG, the sort of girl who is clearly trying to bag a pro footballer. It was obvious what she wanted from me, and I was more than happy to oblige!

She was tall, slim and very sexy and Mel and I were

equally attracted to her. We decided it was time for our famous double act. As I escorted her into a taxi I mentioned that Mel was staying with me, and she seemed only too pleased at this news. In fact, on this occasion we didn't have to use any subterfuge to have our wicked way with her. When Mel came into my bedroom to find us already well down to business, she simply said in her sexy, soft voice, 'Hi Mel, come and join us!' He was grinning from ear to ear, and I'm sure I was too.

This was one of those nights when you are only too glad to go into extra time. But I did have a shock when she suddenly produced a camera from her bag and started taking flash photos of us. I thought perhaps we had made a terrible mistake and my ugly mug was going to be splashed across the tabloids a couple of days later, but nothing like that happened. Perhaps we were just another pair of trophies to add to her list of soccer conquests. When she happily paid £100 for a cab to take her to Windsor, I thought this was a woman who loved the high life and could afford it.

We had fun telling Abby and the boys about our three-in-a-bed night of lust the next day.

My nephews Lewis and Nathan would watch one or two games down at Brisbane Road and I was beginning to nurture hopes that one day they would have the chance to follow in my footsteps.

After a successful first season with Orient, I blotted my copybook by letting my opinionated attitude get me into hot water with the management, particularly my manager, Pat Holland. So in my second season I took a break and spent a month on loan to Colchester, just to experience a different environment. When I returned, Pat called me in for a chat. He told me that Second Division club Watford now wanted me on loan with the possibility of a permanent transfer. With Watford being two divisions higher, this presented an opportunity to climb back up the ladder again and get back my former high profile status.

Although I was excited at this prospect, what I really wanted was an immediate transfer, and you can guess why – I badly needed another fat cheque. I was of course still heavily in debt because of my gambling. Clearing my debt was my priority and to do that I had to think short term – I just wanted another payday. But there was no cheque on the table – just the offer of a month's loan to prove my worth. It seems inconceivable that anyone would turn down such an opportunity, but I did. In the end, my greed and my need for big bucks outweighed my desire to invest in my career. I remember talking to Luther Blissett, ex-England and AC Milan striker, who was on the coaching staff of Watford, who was baffled that I was turning down their offer. I didn't tell him my real reasons.

So the next Saturday, instead of playing for Watford against Sunderland at Vicarage Road, I was playing an away match against Mansfield. After getting over his initial shock Pat accepted me back into the fold and I continued with Orient.

Still drowning in debt and with no sign of that lucrative new contract on the horizon, I was now wondering how I was going to dig my way out of the debt mountain my gambling had given me. I now owed over £100,000 in loans, credit cards and personal debts, along with shortfalls in properties I owned in Stoke and Coventry which would have taken it to more than £300,000 in total. The worry was making me stressed and withdrawn. I had never felt this way before and it was becoming quite scary.

Just to give you an idea how bad things were by the mid 1990s, I opened a phone account at Corals so I could bet 24 hours a day. It gave me access to bets on any sport I fancied. All I had to do was pick up my mobile and I could lose £50 on anything from golf tournaments to tennis matches. I even became addicted to listening to commentaries over the phone – at premium call rates. The result was that I ran up astronomical phone bills. Soon I would be chasing losses just to pay the phone bill – if that isn't being a mug I don't know what is. With my mind already scrambled and my sanity on the edge, I would pace around the room, my phone glued to my ear, hollering for my horse to win. More often than not I would end up throwing my phone at the wall in disgust. I got through quite a few phones during those years.

Nothing, however, beats the comfort of a warm betting shop. Sitting in there perched on a leather-covered stool with a hot coffee in my hand felt like heaven. Of course, it soon turned into hell.

In 1996, to add another complication to my chaotic life, Sandra told me she was pregnant. Our relationship was still very much on and off, but despite this I was delighted. I certainly couldn't have asked for a nicer or better woman to be the mother of my child. There had been some highs and lows, some happy times and sad times along my journey, but being at the birth of my beautiful daughter Savanna on August 27 1997 was something I will always cherish. I will never as long as I live forget seeing her little face for the first time.

The birth of a first child is always a special moment, and it certainly was for me. My feelings of love and pride just couldn't be put into words.

Having said that, it gave me a huge scare when the hospital phoned at one in the morning to tell me to get down there as it was all happening. I raced through the streets of Enfield at 80 mph, jumping red lights and screeching round corners. I got there in time, but I was a nervous wreck!

I now faced a difficult decision. I had realised it was time to say goodbye to the world of professional football. This was no spur-of-the-moment decision – I had been realising for some time that as far as my football career was concerned the only way for me now was down. I wanted to change my life, to get on top of my gambling addiction and spend more time with Sandra and our lovely new daughter.

So in January 1998 my nine-year career as a pro came to an end. Unfortunately my last meeting with

Barry Hearn did not go as planned. There was six months to go on my contract and I asked to be paid up to the end of it, which would have meant £15,000 in my hand, but Barry was too sharp for my agent and I ended up walking out of the office with a cheque for £7500. Mugged – you bet I was! Yet to be honest, strange as it sounds, I was relieved. I just wanted to start a new life as soon as possible.

I had offers on the table and postponed my retirement by going to play for Falkirk FC in the Scottish First Division, but a month in Falkirk would be enough for anyone's sanity – talk about grim, not to mention the freezing weather! I swiftly returned to London and dumped my agent. After securing a two-year contract with my old club St Albans I continued as a semi-pro and got a job as a custody officer, and with my wages from that and £300 a week from St Albans, kicking off with a £3000 signing fee, I was feeling quite contented. The money enabled me to get some of the vultures off my back – for a while at least.

My priority now was to make sure I could look after my little princess Savanna, and I decided to seek help with my gambling addiction. After a meeting with the PFA, talks with family members and a few counselling sessions, I was beginning to come to terms with my problem. They say the urge to bet never leaves you, and although I was doing my best to overcome it I certainly gave into it on a few occasions. When I needed a fix I would be off in the motor down the M1 to the Staley Casino in Coventry. I actually had some good nights there and I remember going with Sandra one night and winning £800. Maybe I should have taken her more often!

But nights like that were few and far between. More often than not I would be hanging on to my last £20 note, just to make sure I could get back home.

Although my mum and dad and the rest of the family showed great concern over my addiction and gave me support and advice, they never really knew the full extent of my problem. I didn't want to worry them any more than I had to, and of course I felt a deep sense of shame.

It was Sandra who suggested that I should seek counselling for my problem. I'm pleased to say I took her advice, and found a counsellor on the internet. At first I feared it would be a waste of time, but I was wrong. Kate proved to be a gentle, softly-spoken woman who obviously knew what she was doing. She encouraged me to talk, and soon I could hardly stop!

I broke down when I started pouring out the details of my gambling addiction. She assured me that we have to go through the bad to get to the good. She promised me that a happier future was in store if I could only learn to help myself. She was so patient, and such a great listener. It was as if I was talking to a sister.

My hour with Kate flew by, and by the time it was over I felt hugely relieved that I had finally got my problem into the open. I went on to have two more appointments with her, and felt much stronger at the end of it. Finally I felt I could move forward and start building a better future.

As I look back at my pro career I feel I do understand where I went wrong, and that is very important. Many pro soccer players finish their careers without appreciating their own mistakes, and start feeling sorry for themselves and becoming bitter. They often find it hard to cope with coming back down to the real world, because football is all they have known. It's not hard to understand how a retired footballer can self-destruct, even turn to crime, because they have had the one thing that really mattered to them taken away. You have to count your blessings for having had the chance, and find a way of replacing your career with something else. Fortunately for me I was very much in the real world for some years before I turned pro, so readjusting was relatively easy, although it was still hard work coming to terms with the return to ordinary life.

Today's flash young players need to appreciate that the celebrity lifestyle of the pro footballer comes with a big health warning. If you don't take any notice, you will soon be heading for disaster. Sacrifices have to be made, and listening to those close to you is of paramount importance.

My most important piece of advice I can give to the young footballer is about money. It is vital you start saving or investing some of it right from the outset, because it won't be there for ever. Before you know it you are thirty years old and skint!

When I talk to fifteen and sixteen-year-olds today I try to get across how important hard work and dedication are to making it in soccer. You don't have to be the most talented player in the team, whichever team it is, from the school playground to your local Sunday league. But you do have to be prepared to work your socks off for the team. As long as you can offer 100 per cent dedication you have a chance. Talent and ability are very important, but without effort and commitment you will not make the grade. On my scouting missions I see many semi-pro players of 18 or 19 who think they are good enough to go professional, but they fail to realise that a little talent with the ball and a propensity to 'showboat' do not make you a professional footballer. There's a lot of hard work between being talented and being successful.

My son Shane, who is now 17, has ambitions to follow in my footsteps, but I keep trying to drum it into his head that every time he steps on to that pitch he needs to give a hundred per cent. I hope one day he will make the grade, but I am not pushing him to get there too quickly. If he is good enough and adopts the right attitude, one day it will happen.

My roller-coaster journey through football has been amazing, and I feel privileged to have fulfilled my dream. When I look back at my videos, DVDs and newspaper cuttings with my kids I'm proud of what I achieved, and with more dedication and a better attitude I know it could have been more rewarding. The demons I failed to conquer were my downfall,

During my two years at St Albans Mel and I became agents. We even managed to get our cousin Leon a pro contract with Cambridge United. I enjoyed doing this as a part-time business, but I wasn't able to turn it into a full-time career because I took a full-time job with Network Rail in 2000. I did use my contacts to make a few deals, and could easily return to that side of the game in the future.

One day when I was driving my cousin Leon down to Ilkeston Town FC to seal a transfer, ex-England Captain Mark Wright called me on my mobile. He tried to hijack the deal and persuade Leon to sign for his Chester City side, but I stood firm and even his £3000 sweetener was not enough to change my mind. Not surprisingly Mark seemed rather stunned. The fact was I did not care who it was on the end of the phone at that point, as I simply wanted to make sure I looked after my cousin - not to mention the fact that I did not want to do a U-turn on the deal we had with Ilkeston.

I remember watching a lad from Kosovo called Nibeel and contacting my ex-team mate Glen Cockerill (ex Southampton star) and asking him to take a look at him. Glen was then manager of Woking, who were riding high in the Conference League. After a couple of training sessions and a long chat with Glen, he turned round and said "Fuck me, where did you get this lad from? He's a star!" There was not much more to be said other than to sort out Nibeel's contract. Glen agreed a one-year deal at £200 per week (no tax) just to see how he was, as he was a very raw 18-year-old and couldn't even speak English.

Nibeel had to go back to his digs, or so I thought. I knew he was trying to secure his stay in England. Then I got a call from someone who said he was Nibeel's key worker. "Sorry Tony, but Nibeel is about to be deported" he said.

I was gutted for Nibeel, as he had so much promise. The terms the club were able to offer were not enough to keep him in the UK. It was such a shame, as that lad could have been a star.

My playing days were now slowly but surely coming to an end. The next contract I signed, with Harlow Town FC, would be my last. I spent 18 months at Harlow and met some great people. In the end I was offered the reserve team manager's job, but I was never one for management. In 1999, aged 35, I hung up my boots for the last time.

CHAPTER 8

Looking Back

Once I had hung up my boots for good, I found I had time at last to reflect on my experiences and my many adventures in the world of football. We all hear horror stories of ex-professional footballers who can't cope with life out of the limelight and find living in the real world a challenge. Some very famous names have found life after soccer extremely difficult to deal with and embarked on the road to self-destruction.

I heard that one of the lads I had played with at Bristol City was struggling so much with life after football that he ended up doing a four-year stretch in prison, and I'm sure he's not the only one. His name was Andy Llewellyn, and as I had been close to him in those Bristol City days I really felt for him. After all this was a man who played professional football for over fifteen years and represented his country at the highest level.

When you have thrown yourself into the game with

all your heart and soul and suddenly find it is not in your life any more, it is very difficult to fill the void left behind. Even if you have managed to retire with your wealth intact, what can you do to replace your life on the pitch? No more guest lists and VIP treatment, no more scantily-clad beauties going weak at the knees because you're a famous footballer, no more adulation by the home crowd on a Saturday afternoon, no more crazy card schools and friendly banter on the coach trips. And worst of all – no more giant pay cheques!

When you are used to splashing out bundles of cash every weekend, it's quite a shock to the system when the purse strings have to be tightened. At least I came from an working background, so I was able to leave pro football in the knowledge that I was returning to my former life, so to speak, and that was something I was able to deal with. Sadly, many ex-colleagues of mine have not had that safety net to fall back on. It seems that if you have known nothing else but the world of pro football and then suddenly have it taken away from you, it can be impossible to adapt to normal life. Some are plunged into depression, or turn to crime or drink. From where I'm sitting that is totally understandable. I miss my glory days dreadfully, but at least I'm lucky enough to have a good family to help me move on and leave it behind.

So I managed to settle into a new life away from the fame and the glory, helping Sandra to raise our daughter, but guess what – I was still indulging in my favourite pastime. I was no longer a gambling addict, but I couldn't resist the odd flutter. I still paid the odd visit to Stanley Casino in Coventry – and just when I thought I was kicking the habit, they started bringing in new technology to lure me back in. Plasma screens and plush seats were installed, so it was more comfortable than ever to sit back reading the *Sporting Life* and selecting your bets for the day. The new generation of betting shops had hit our streets in a big way, and the invitation to come inside and have a flutter was irresistible. For me, like so many others, this spelled disaster.

Gambling had now become a multi-million dollar industry. And now along came on-line gambling – available in the home 24/7.

I did manage to cut down my gambling, mainly because of my children and my responsibility to them. That isn't to say I didn't still enjoy a bet. The gambling urge might be suppressed, but it never goes away.

While some can move on, others find it just too difficult. The only answer is to plan ahead, to make sure you have a life after football. When the bubble bursts and you wake up one morning feeling redundant and lost, the feeling can lead to all sort of psychological and physical problems. Suddenly the school run or the Saturday afternoon shopping becomes a regular chore and that sense of emptiness can become unbearable. That's why some sportsmen end up on the path of no return.

I just hope my story will hit home with the thousands of youngsters out there who dream of one day walking out on to the pitch at Anfield or Old Trafford. I hope managers, teachers, coaches and mentors – as well as parents – will read my story and use it as example of the challenges professional football can throw at you. You have to be prepared to be dedicated and make sacrifices.

If I could turn the clock back, there is one chapter in my amazing life I would change in an instant. In the spring of 1998 I was enjoying the taste of success in my football career, but I was drowning in debt and besieged by debt collectors banging on my door. Such was my predicament that I would have frankly have done pretty much anything to earn a quick buck, regardless of the consequences. Mel and I put our heads together and I rang a contact of mine on a tabloid newspaper and told him I was prepared to do a 'kiss and tell' in return for suitable payment. I'd heard of huge payouts being made by this newspaper in return for juicy gossip about famous people, and couldn't resist the chance to make some money. So on Sunday April 19 that year, I picked up the phone.

Without going into any detail, the person we so shamelessly used was a woman we knew, a well-known TV actress. Of course the newspaper sleazed it up, and by the time they had finished with it it made pretty appalling reading, though no doubt it was amusing for the readers. I feel terrible regret to think of the damage I did to that woman, all because of my desperate need for money, thanks to the curse of my gambling addiction. Our story was splashed across the pages of a national newspaper. It gave us a buzz at the time, but it was a selfish act which should not have happened, something which no human being should feel the need to do. I'm pleased to say the woman we wronged has since gone from strength to strength in her career – in fact I think we even helped to raise her profile. It's ironic that I am a firm believer in 'karma' and believe what goes around comes around, and that what happened to me afterwards was no more than I deserved. The few thousand pounds we received didn't last either – now there's a surprise!

Of course, I should never have picked up the phone and made that call. I have since had fifteen years to mull over my wrongdoing and now that God is in my life I know I can hope for forgiveness – I just hope the woman I wronged can feel the same way.

Lurking around the corner was a gigantic blow – the death of my dad at the age of only 67. I had never experienced the loss of a loved one until we lost him on March 10th 2002. He had been diagnosed with cancer two years earlier. I don't want to dwell on Dad's death and the pain he suffered, as I would much rather keep my memories of him as he was when he was strong and well.

The last football match he ever saw me play in was an FA Trophy match in front of a large crowd against Woking at Clarence Park (our home ground). We drew 1-1. My pal Greg Howell managed to equalise in the last minute with a penalty in front of the 800-strong crowd of St Albans faithful. That was a relief, as I didn't want to walk off that pitch having lost the game after playing a blinder, and with Dad and Mel watching.

After the match I sat in the players' bar and watched Dad sipping his pint. Every couple of minutes he gave me another compliment on my performance (I have to say I was top man that day, thank goodness, and I have the video to prove it!)

Dad's smiles and laughter that day stay with me, as do the love and support he shared with me throughout my football career, going right back to that magical day when he drove me and Mel to our first training session with Coundon Cockerels in his VW camper van. Those memories are priceless.

Dad never hesitated to tell me about it if I hadn't played so well either, as in the last time he saw me play professionally, for Leyton Orient against Wycombe Wanderers in 1998. But it was great to see Mum and my niece Nina cheering me on.

With Dad gone, football out of my life and still struggling to get out of a mountain of debt, life in the new millennium was not looking great. I think what kept me strong, and the family too, was the strength we all gained from my sister Patricia. She is the organiser of the family, and her words of wisdom and strong faith have kept us all on an even keel and helped us to come to terms with our trials.

No sooner had I come to terms with Dad's death

than I suffered another heartbreak, one that came as far more of a shock and turned my world, and that of the whole family, upset down.

On the night of April 9 2004 I was sitting in Sandra's house chilling out when the phone rang. Even today the memory of that call sends a chill through me. It was Mel, and he had a two-word message: 'Ian's gone'. My older brother, big strong Ian, had died in St Vincent.

It was a total shock. Ian wasn't ill or anything, and he was only 47. Apparently he had drowned, though it was obvious there had been more to his death than an accident. He was the best swimmer in the family and extremely fit. He was born in St Vincent and its roughest waters were paddling pools to him.

I was in a daze and felt numb. All I could do was pace up and down chain-smoking furiously, my heart pounding as I tried to take on board what had happened. I felt alone and lost, as Mel was in Coventry and Sandra and Savanna were in Barbados. I called Sandra and told her the news. If only she had been there to hold me instead of three thousand miles away.

Mel eventually turned up at the flat and told me the story in more detail. Later the whole family went to St Vincent to try to find out what had really happened, and we soon got to the bottom of it. Ian had not drowned at all, though the authorities insisted he had.

Ian had been living with an extremely possessive girlfriend who was, as they say, 'not all there'. On one occasion she hit him over the head with a beer bottle.

We all told him he was with a madwoman, but our warnings fell on deaf ears. Unfortunately she happened to be rich, having inherited a large sum of money from her late gangster husband. Money talks of course, so when she wanted to cover up the real reason for his death she just slipped some cash to the authorities. It seems Ian was poisoned before he had been put into the water. We hoped to try to prove it, but in the end it was clear we would be wasting our money.

As an ex-Army man Ian had no fear – whenever I was in his company I felt totally safe. He left three daughters behind – Charlotte, Dominique and Nina – and a son, Kristen. I felt for all of them as they had to come to terms with the way they had lost their dad so suddenly and tragically. As usual Patricia was a tower of strength. Although I had evil thoughts of revenge in my mind, I had to put them aside and grieve for my brother. I was strongly tempted to seek revenge for Ian's death, and we had a family conference to discuss what to do about it. My mother quite rightly insisted that we should never stoop to such evil ourselves and should trust in our faith. God would look after things, she said. Much as I wanted to right this terrible injustice, I knew she was right. It was best to leave things in God's hands.

We all wonder why tragedies happen and why good people suffer, but I believe today that everything happens for a reason - we just don't know what that reason is. All I know is that God stepped in to stop us behaving recklessly out of anger and keep us out of jail.

Throughout my life I had been coming across adversity in some form, and I wondered what was next. I was struggling mentally and suffering repeated flashbacks in the aftermath of Ian's death. I'm pleased to say that what followed was a happier and more comforting experience, and one which has helped to make me what I am today. Just when I was in despair in the aftermath of Ian's death, still struggling to deal with my debt and still confused over my relationship with Sandra, my own light at the end of the tunnel was provided by the chaplain at Network Rail.

The moment he arrived at my signal box one sunny Monday afternoon, I felt at ease. I felt a guardian angel had come along to direct me on to the right path and take away the stress, pain and evil thoughts I was feeling. It wasn't so much that I found God, just that I felt I had someone to guide me at last. We sat and talked for an hour, and after he left I felt my mind had been cleared. A huge weight had been lifted from my shoulders. All the bleak negativity had gone and my whole outlook on life had become more positive.

Fortunately my faith is now strong enough to enable me to deal with the adversity life throws at me. Religion may not be for everyone, but it works for me. It has opened my mind to the world we live in today.

Now that I have started down the path of redemption I am trying to put something back, in any way I can. I hope to help young 'wannabe' footballers by advising them and educating them in what it means to play the game at pro level.

For me it's important that I acknowledge my mistakes, and with that comes a sense of contentment, as I know that through the mistakes I have made I have affected many people's lives in a negative way. Now I want to undo the damage by making a positive contribution to the lives of others.

As soon as I had had that talk with the chaplain, I felt a new sense of direction and a new feeling of stability. I went on to have regular meetings with him to listen to his calming words and receive his guidance.

In 2006 I managed to buy a new flat in North London, and that was when Sandra and I finally decided to call time on our on-off relationship after nearly 20 years. We were still the best of friends, and our focus is on our daughter and making sure she grows up in a happy and stable environment. She is the reason Sandra and I will always be best friends, even though we are no longer together. Sandra has had to endure all my trials and tribulations with me – the womanising, the card schools, the betting shops, the money troubles, the triumphs and tragedies, but she has always been there for me, which is why I hold her in such high regard. She is a wonderful woman.

At last I had now finally beaten my demon – or at least, 95 per cent. I don't think I could ever give up having the odd bet. My faith, my growing responsibilities and those who gave me professional advice finally enabled me to rid myself of this devastating disease – and it is a disease. I lost a lot of money, but at least I still have my health, my home and a lovely family.

My personal journey into crisis reached its climax in August 2010, when I finally plucked up the courage to file for bankruptcy. It was then that I knew I had finally hit rock bottom. After years of misery and pain I had somehow racked up debts amounting to a total of £169,000. I know exactly how much it was, because with the help of a debt counselling agency I sat down and compiled all the paperwork.

Declaring bankruptcy is a huge step, and it is not as straightforward as it might sound. There was a mountain of paperwork involved, but the debt agency were very good and in return for the sum of £600 they helped me to sort it all out. They also helped me to get a huge weight off my shoulders.

In a strange way I was quite excited about the prospect of going bankrupt, because at last I could see a way out of my troubles and the possibility of a debt-free future. But first I had to get through the High Court process, which involves making a clean breast of everything, including precise details of all your debts and assets, and then declaring before a judge at a formal hearing that you are unable to pay your debts.

On the day, Mel accompanied me to the hearing at the High Court. As we stepped off the tube my mind began to race. Although I was feeling hopeful and positive, there was the obvious apprehensiveness as to what the day would bring. God knows what I would do if they refused to make me bankrupt – I would have to soldier on somehow with my crushing mountain of debt.

I handed over my file and my £600 application fee to the clerk and began to sweat it out as I waited to be called. It felt as if I was on death row. I was told to return at 2 pm for the judgment, and it was the longest three hours of my life. I couldn't begin to imagine what I would do if the judge was not prepared to grant my bankruptcy.

Finally we reported back to the court and were told to go upstairs to the Bankruptcy Decisions Office. When the clerk uttered the words 'Your bankruptcy petition has been accepted' I felt an enormous surge of relief. It was as if I had suddenly been cleansed in some way. Ironically, it was the same feeling I had when I'd had a big gambling win!

But this really was a big win – in fact, in a sense, it was the biggest win of my life. Mel and I just looked at each other and he gave me a wry smile. He didn't have to say anything – he knew what this meant to me. I was now, so to speak, a free man, and could get on with rebuilding my life.

As I stepped outside the court all the pent-up emotion I was feeling inside came pouring out. I felt elated. Needless to say, the next stop was the nearest pub. At last I had something to celebrate. The rest of the afternoon remains a blur to this day.

So how had I managed to end up £169,000 in debt after eight and a half years as a well-paid pro footballer?

When I try to explain to my colleagues at work they find it hard to understand, and I don't blame them. But the reality is that I am far from alone. The problem is made worse by the gambler's reluctance to admit he had a problem – as with alcoholism. The irony is that most gamblers get into their addiction because they want to 'get rich quick', yet that is exactly the opposite of what happens, as my story demonstrates. You do have the big wins and the days when it all seems to be going your way, but the bookies always come out on top in the end. If you want to live your life with money to spend, stay away from them!

With my life moving in a better direction, I have continued my involvement in soccer. I work at the Tottenham Hotspur training ground, helping to look after corporate security, hosting and surveillance. I deal with the press and the players. I find this a very satisfying job which keeps me happily involved in the game I love. In time I hope to work with the PFA to help them rid of the game of the curse of gambling.

I am also involved in scouting for talent. I have my own 'contract' which I use when I find a player I can pass on to my contacts. I will soon be taking up a role in a 'soccer college' in London and hope to help the kids there, who range from 12-18 years – not just in developing their soccer skills but in facing the challenges of the footballing life which I faced, particularly, of course, the gambling demon.

One day, out of the blue, I had a pleasant surprise.

In April 2009 I had a call from Stoke City, inviting me to be their guest of honour at a match against Newcastle United at the Britannia Stadium. Not only was I given the best seats in the house and treated to a slap-up meal, along with a guest – I took my brother Abby - but I was paid a fee for attending. Abby and I made a night of it by meeting up with the old crew and having a wild night out.

When I walked on to the pitch at half time I got a wonderful ovation. I felt honoured to be remembered in this way, and spending time after the match signing autographs outside the ground brought back fond memories of my days with the club. It was a magic feeling, though not surprisingly it was tinged with sadness, as it reminded me what I had been missing.

I will always have a soft spot for Stoke, the club that gave me my greatest-ever night on a football pitch. I will certainly be a lifelong supporter.

I'm not resting on my laurels - my redemption is not complete yet. I'm still trying hard to be the person I want to be and not the person I was. My kids, now 16 and 17, both know what their dad has been through and are proud of my achievements on the football pitch, which is all that matters to me. Shane and Savanna are my priority now, and I'm sure they will make their dad proud of them in whatever they choose to do – football, I hope, in Shane's case. He is doing very well, playing right wing, the same position I started in. And like me, he is lightning fast!

He is now with semi-pro club Wingate and Finchley FC, with the reserves/youth team. When he hits 18 I plan to use my contacts to send him on trial and see if I can secure a pro contract for him so he can follow in his dad's footsteps. Time will tell.

In 2011 I left Network Rail to focus on work in various fields of security, and you may even come across me booted and suited standing in the doorway of a London night club! My main work is in corporate security. I hope to continue scouting for soccer talent. I also intend to continue my writing and plan to start a new project shortly.

This has been a long journey, one filled with joy and heartache, pain and glory, despair and hope, heartache and love. And I'm still in my forties!

I don't know how I would have managed without all the people who have stood by me and supported and helped me. We all need our friends and family to get through this crazy life.

My main purpose in writing this book is to do what I can to help today's up and coming young footballers to get it right and not to make the mistakes I made and follow my path to near ruin. I hope to do all I can to help and advise the next generation.

To anyone who is thinking of getting into the world of pro football, remember that it's not a holiday from real life, it's a job, and like any job you need to do it conscientiously and to the best of your ability. Like any job, it can end at any time if things go wrong, whether it's your fault or not. In fact it's a good deal less secure than many jobs because your continued employment depends on performing 100 per cent.

Today, gone are the dolly birds and the fast cars, the moments of glory and fame, the wild nights out, the thrills and spills on the pitch, the dressing-room banter – and most of all, gone are the fat pay packets. But I have other things to take comfort from – my family and friends, my new job, my home and my continued involvement in football.

If this story saves just one young footballing prodigy from self-destruction, it will have been worthwhile.